THE GUIDE
TO LEGALLY
OBTAINING
A FOREIGN
PASSPORT

THE EASY WAY TO GET
ADDITIONAL CITIZENSHIPS

THE GUIDE TO LEGALLY OBTAINING A FOREIGN PASSPORT

THE EASY WAY TO GET ADDITIONAL CITIZENSHIPS

D. O'Nes

SHAPOLSKY PUBLISHERS, INC.
NEW YORK

A Shapolsky Book

For any additional information, contact:
Shapolsky Publishers, Inc.
136 West 22nd Street, New York, NY 10011

2, 3, 4, 5, 6, 7, 8, 9, 10

ISBN 0-944007-93-7 (paper)

Book Design and Typography by The Bartlett Press, Inc.,
Somerset, New Jersey

This book is dedicated to the many people who helped:
my supportive parents, Mina and Carol,
my talented editors Fred Salaf, Roy and Anat,
all the friends who challenged me to write this book,
all the government officials who patiently cooperated
with my research efforts, Josef Silver, the brilliant immigration
lawyer who provided me with invaluable insights,
and lastly and most importantly,
to Dov Nesis—without whom this book
would never have been possible.

Contents

PART II

Introduction

This guide is a result of extensive research and market analysis which confirms that a new breed of entrepreneurs has emerged, keen on taking advantage of the many opportunities that doing business overseas affords. These entrepreneurs are thirsty for new information which can assist them in seeking financial and personal rewards. They believe that the world is fast becoming a global economic village and they want to be part of it.

But up to now, one of the stumbling blocks to achieving success in this international business environment has been elusive because information has been scarce, unreliable and confusing. Now, for the first time ever in print, the vital and totally reliable information is offered to assist all those who are ready to accept the challenge and change their lives.

The Guide to Legally Obtaining a Foreign Passport contains information which anyone can follow. Join those who have already taken the path to success and, indeed, have conquered new worlds!

In *The Guide to Legally Obtaining a Foreign Passport* you will learn that an additional passport permits you to work and conduct business in different countries which do not enjoy close or "preferred" relations with your own country. It is often desirable to conceal one's real nationality for the purposes of doing business overseas or for personal security.

Holding a second, foreign passport could actually save your life in the event of a hijacking, kidnaping, or military or civil disturbance which could threaten your personal safety. Many revolutionary groups, unstable governments, or even terrorists will seek out citizens of a particular country to use as hostages. Many of these hostages, of course, might even be killed.

The second passport idea is not new. The thousands of savvy people who already have one obtained theirs the hard way. They had to struggle to find the information and loopholes that are presented here for the first time. One of the prime reasons they were so keen on getting a second, "golden" passport was to be able to save on taxes! By becoming a citizen of a country with low taxation, the entrepreneur can truly enjoy financial freedom.

Holding citizenship and a passport of a foreign country gives you the option of eventual immigration there. Since this guide is written for readers with a broad range of requirements around the world, this thought is comforting.

The same loopholes in acquiring foreign citizenship are available to almost all peoples of the world.

Immigration to another country permits one to shed the obligations and duties, and perhaps oppression found in the "home" country. In other terms, immigration to another country by means of legally obtained citizenship and a passport could allow the avoidance of tax authorities, legal authorities, or any other possible obligations and complications.

An Obtainable Goal

The road to obtaining the citizenship and passport of another country is a rocky one, but well worth it. The process can take up to ten years and consists of two fundamental and interactive actions.

The first requirement in the process is the application for permanent residency in a "new" country. In some instances, acquiring permanent residency is sufficient to meet one's needs.

The second step is the acquiring of citizenship status. There is a waiting period, usually up to 5 years from the time that the permanent residency is granted before an application for citizenship can be filed. This system is fairly uniform throughout all countries.

Once the application for permanent residency has been filed, a prolonged residence in the intended country is some times required. It is during this period of residency that an applicant's actions are taken in to account by the authorities in the final determination in granting citizenship.

If your intended purpose is emigration to another country, the time spent in that country required for permanent residency status will not be objectionable. However, if you want to own a foreign passport without spending a very lengthy residency period in your "chosen" country then you will want to eliminate from your list of potential countries all those whose residency requirements are inconvenient.

Holland has officially declared, for instance, that it is not a typical immigration country. Therefore, permanent residence there is extremely difficult to achieve.

In Norway there is a ban on immigration and no residency permits or working documents for foreigners of any nationality are issued.

Here are two enlightened European countries with impenetrable immigration barriers which illustrate just how difficult the problem is. Switzerland holds the record for those countries allowing immigration: 10 years of continuous permanent residency before an application for citizenship can be accepted!

Three governing bodies must approve the applicant: The Swiss Federal government, the canton's government, and the local municipality. And there is no guarantee that citizenship will ever be granted at the end of the ten year process!

Austria grants citizenship after ten years of permanent residency, as does Iceland, Spain, and the Philippines.

The aim of this guide is to provide you with information about obtaining an additional foreign passport by employing reasonable methods and time. The goal is certainly obtainable and efforts will be well rewarded.

The world is divided into 180 independent governmental units which share common characteristics in many aspects concerning immigration. Each country's laws governing immigration have evolved from the traditions, localized circumstances, and ideologies which were instrumental in forming a national identity. There are some countries which grew out of immigration, and have a more open policy as a result, towards new immigration. Some countries, because of external and/or internal situations have closed their borders. Others are growing alarmed at the growth of their population and have acted to stem the flow of immigration.

Even in the face of such potential obstacles, loopholes exist to open the right doors. These "chinks in the armor" have allowed clever entrepreneurs to circumvent and outwit, in entirely legal ways, the normally taken routes in obtaining foreign citizenship.

There are a number of countries which have an "open door" immigration policy. Primarily to provide a boost to their economy, these countries welcome investors who infuse large amounts of cash into the nation's coffers. Citizenship and a passport in the "recipient" country is a small price to pay in return for the potential cash flow provided by high rolling investors, developers, business persons and entrepreneurs.

This guide contains tips about the "international passport industry" that will benefit the average reader. The guide will also reveal short cuts in the passport application process which can result in the saving of time and money. These short cuts will lead the reader through the legal and often bureaucratic stumbling blocks. And they will allow the passport seeker to obtain more than what was originally expected.

For the purposes of simplicity, we are going to split the world into groups. First are what we call the "classic" immigration countries: Australia, New Zealand, Canada, and the United States. Another group comprises the European Common Market countries, which, by and large, do not readily grant citizenship and issue passports. In fact, these countries do not encourage immigration at all. Possessing a passport from Italy, Ireland, Belgium, United Kingdom, Germany, Holland, Greece, Luxembourg, Spain, Portugal, or France is very convenient. Passports issued by these countries have many unique advantages and benefits, which will be covered later in this book. In northern Europe there are the Scandinavian countries—Denmark, Norway, Sweden, Finland, and Iceland which also grant many benefits to passport holders.

All the groups mentioned above are part of the "North vs. South," as Willi Brandt, former West German Chancellor coined the term for rich, first World countries. On the other end of the spectrum is the "South," which obviously stands for poorer and third World countries.

But our categorization takes a different bent: The developed, Western nations comprise the First World, the East European and Asian Communist Bloc comprise the Second World, and the rest of the countries comprise the Third World. In this last category are most of the Asiatic, African, Central and South American countries. In this group 125 countries are included. Some have recently attained independence, and others have been around a long time.

There is no doubt that the most desired passports are the ones from the First World because people who wish to emigrate usually prefer to settle in one of the countries comprising this group. However, many enlightened entrepreneurs prefer a Third World country's passport because they do not wish to emigrate or live in one of the countries in this group; only to reap the benefits offered.

In the summer of 1986 London's Stock Exchange altered the system of exchange by enabling continuous transactions 24 hours a day, from Tokyo to New York. This change was expected, especially by those who are in international business and who are usually always on the go. They jet across continents, and either spend a great deal of time abroad or actually live abroad, working in overseas offices. This connection in and to a foreign country strengthens their business ties and investment opportunities. The frequent bond established by the business traveler and a foreign land justly requires an additional passport which could result in smoother business dealings, transactions, and profits. The big question is how to *legally* obtain the second passport. Many fail in their attempts to acquire one. Some get "burned" by using a false passport or fraudulent documentation.

One example of a how otherwise knowledgeable and intelligent people become involved in passport schemes is the case of a certain dictator of a Third World country who, over a ten year period, issued hundreds of certified passports to anyone who could afford his astronomical asking price. It was only a matter of time until the dictator was overthrown and all the passports he issued were invalidated by his successor.

In their zeal to achieve the benefits which having a second, but genuine passport would bring, many, otherwise law abiding people sometimes resort to illegal means. In the end it's usually the same—embarrassment, possible jail sentence, loss of large amounts of money and time. These people did not know there was another way!

The information provided in this guide will help avoid any legal pitfalls. Useful names and addresses are listed throughout for further follow-up.

After reading this guide you will have acquired important new information which you will find useful, even if you are not an investor. There is no doubt, however, that your interest will be aroused. The information has been gathered from various open and frank sources from around the world. Some of our informants are diplomatic representatives, and every document has been checked for authenticity. However, the author cautions the reader to take into account the ever-changing world political scene which can cause otherwise timely and reliable information to become obsolete. Additionally, this guide gives a general overview to the subject.

Neither recommendations nor moral judgments are not implied or given. The reader should utilize the information found in this guide as a stepping stone, proceeding cautiously and with common sense at all times.

Investments and Passports

Numerous countries grant permanent residency quite readily to those who are prepared to invest significant, but reasonable amounts of capital. Permanent residency leads to citizenship, which, in turn, leads to the acquisition of a passport. Some countries issue a full citizenship status, almost immediately and almost automatically, to those who meet certain investment criteria. In some countries a deposit in a local bank is sufficient, and is regarded as a qualified investment.

Other countries seek investors for an active business which will create jobs. Priority is given, in many instances, to investors who rescue bankrupt businesses. Still other countries grant citizenship to large real estate investors. The degree of desirability of a particular country's passport often determines the minimum required for investment.

Each application by a potential investor is handled on a purely individual basis. Applications can be scrutinized to determine if the sources of investment are tarnished. However, more likely, is the overlooking of any dubious sources as the foreign country usually is in great need for the cash, jobs or other benefits that the investment will bring. Wise investors are usually able to recoup their original capital fairly quickly.

Approved and Non-Approved Investments in Foreign Countries

The application is submitted to the auditor of foreign currency in the Federal Reserve Bank in the country of origin, for approval of the withdrawal of foreign currency. (This is not required in all countries). The application is presented to an inter-bureau committee which is comprised of representatives of the Bureau of Commerce and Industry and members of the budget directors of that country. Generally, the committee approves the withdrawal of foreign currency on condition that it will benefit national interests as well as private ones.

Except for suspicion of private profiteering, the application is normally approved by other parameters which can be varied and diverse. For example, a manufacturing plant with good exporting credentials wants to open a subsidiary in another country. Such a venture would enhance the economy in the country of origin because the new plant would be dependent on commodities from the country of origin and would help increase its G.N.P. (gross national product). Sounds perfectly logical—but it doesn't always work. Occasionally, conflicting interests between the two countries in question can present a stumbling block.

You will learn, in the following pages, that there is a way to successfully invest even if your application to export foreign currency is not approved!

PART I

Chapter One
Australia: An Open Door Policy to Prosperity

General Information About the Country

Australia has always been a land of opportunity. As world economics continues its dramatic shift of emphasis towards the Asia/Pacific region, Australia today—and tomorrow—offers an exciting frontier of new challenges and opportunities.

Australia is a continent by itself with wide open spaces. With only an average of two people to every square kilometer, the entire population is a little over 16 million, growing at around 1.5% yearly. Much of this growth comes from immigration. The main centers of population are concentrated along the coast line, in some of the world's most beautiful cities.

Australia has a buoyant and highly developed economy that is enjoying strong growth. Gross domestic product, which currently ranks 8th among OECD Countries (Organization of Economic Cooperation and Development), averaged 4.5% growth over the four years 1984–1987.

Employment has risen by 10% in the last three years and living standards are among the highest in the world. Foreign investment is very welcome.

Australia enjoys a stable political climate. There is a sophisticated consumer market, an educated workforce, and a positive, productive culture. Industry is varied and versatile.

Australia has abundant natural resources and energy. It is the world's largest exporter of coal, iron ore, refined lead, zinc, bauxite, alumina, mineral sands, wool, beef, mutton, and lamb.

For those prepared to identify the market niche that best suits one's interests, particularly strong prospects exists for investment within the industrial and commercial growth sectors. These areas include:

- Aerospace
- Biotechnology and pharmaceuticals
- Chemicals and plastics
- Fibers and ceramics
- Information and communications industries
- New materials, including composites and polymers
- Paper and paper products
- processing of minerals, foodstuffs, wool and hides
- Scientific, education, and medical equipment and services

Australia's financial system is fully internationalized

with no controls on foreign exchange of the flow of funds in or out of the country.

Currency: As of February 1990, the exchange rate for one Australian Dollar is equal to 0.764 of the U.S. Dollar.

Many incentives, aimed particularly at fostering the manufacturing sector, are a strong motivation in their own right for investment in Australia:

- A 150% taxation deduction for expenditure on research and development
- Taxation concessions for certain venture capital investments
- No withholding tax is levied on dividends paid from company income which has borne the standard rate of company tax
- Australia does not levy a branch profits tax
- The standard rate of company tax as of July 1, 1988 is a very competitive 39%
- Export market development grants

Australia is now looking for overseas partners to help develop products and services for world markets.

Questions Often Asked About Australia

Q. What is the average wage?

A. The average weekly wage currently is $A425.00.

Q. How much is income tax?

A. Company tax is 39%

Q. What is retirement age?

A. 65 years for men and 60 years for women

Q. What does health care cost?

A. Australian Medicare entitles every citizen to basic health coverage. A low percentage of income is deducted from all taxable income as a Medicare levy.

Q. What does housing cost?

A. This varies from State to State and city to city. Housing is more expensive in the larger cities like Sydney and Melbourne. The Real Estate Institute of Australia will be able to offer assistance in this area.

Immigration Policy

Australia is one of the very few major developed nations in the world today which is actively welcoming new settlers. Under its active immigration program over 140,000 people will make Australia their home in 1990. In many parts of the world the barriers to immigration are going up. In Australia, they are coming down.

The policy undertaken by the government is aimed at expanding Australia's population while striking a balance between economic, family, and humanitarian needs. There is currently a sharper economic focus on skills and business entry.

Permanent Residence

There are three broad areas in Australia's current immigration policy:

1. The BMP (Business Migration Program)

The objective of the BMP is to attract business people who plan to settle permanently in Australia and contribute heir expertise and capital to ventures which will benefit Australia. These ventures must benefit the country through:

- The creation of employment or retention of jobs which would otherwise be lost
- The stimulation of export trade
- The introduction of new or improved technology
- The replacement of imports

The applicant must have a successful business record and must have sufficient skills and capital to ensure the viability of the business they propose to set up in Australia. They must transfer to Australia money, equipment, or other assets (for example, intellectual property such as patents and trademarks) to the value of at least $A500,000, of which a minimum of $A150,000 must be in cash. The above quoted figures are exclusive of settlement costs. Applicants will be required to demonstrate an understanding of the Australian economy and the feasibility of their project.

The government has accredited BMP agents to assist prospective business immigrants in the preparation of applications, and to carry out the assessment and processing of those applications.

2. The ENS (Employer Nomination Scheme)

The ENS enables Australian employers to seek highly skilled workers from overseas when they have been unable to fill their needs from the Australian labor market.

Under this plan, the emphasis is placed on the employer's recruitment efforts, their training records, and the nominee's skill and experience in relation to their occupations. The objective of this category is to select young, skilled, educated immigrants from a wide range of occupations with the flexibility to meet Australia's broad long term labor market needs.

3. Independent category

Lastly, there is an independent category in which applicants in this category are assessed against an employability criterion that emphasizes skill, age, and English language ability. These are assessed under a "points" system.

The government has introduced a "Floating" Passmarks System for the points assessment. Employability gets the highest weighting. The skill component is measured by a reference to formal education, on the job training, and the likely recognition of the applicant's qualifications in Australia.

4. Special talents

Special consideration is given to people with creative and sporting talent which is of obvious benefit to Australia.

5. Family migration

Those who are sponsored by extended family members in Australia will be assessed under the points system, but they will not be assessed for English. Under this category extended families cover parents, brothers, sisters, non-dependent children, nephews, and nieces.

We gave a more detailed look at Australia, including business opportunities and immigration regulations because in today's world Australia, (with the possible exception of Canada), is the most encouraging towards immigration. We could compare Australia's open door policy today to the United States of the 19th century, a country of truly unlimited potential and opportunities.

The Australian Passport

From the moment you receive the status of permanent resident in Australia, which is a relatively easy task compared to the rest of the world, the road to citizenship is smooth.

After two years of permanent residency status in Australia, you are eligible for an Australian passport. This document is highly regarded throughout the world and is very much in demand. Quite frequently it is compared to the Swiss passport which is considered the most prestigious.

There is an additional advantage that an Australian passport brings; it automatically grants the holder simultaneous residential rights in nearby New Zealand!

It is interesting and important to note that many countries require you to remain, for the required period between permanent resident status and the time you become eligible to apply for citizenship, solely within the borders of their country! Not so with Australia. Although you must spend two years there you may travel outside the country as often as you like. However, the time spent outside the country is not counted towards the two year span needed.

Here is more information which you will find useful:

Inquiries regarding business investment opportunities in Australian should be directed to:

> The Manager
> Investment Enquiries Service
> AUSTRADE
> P.O. Box 2386
> Canberra City ACT AUSTRALIA 2601
> Tel: 062-765258
> Fax: 062-765105

or by contacting an Australian Trade Commission (AUS-TRADE) office in the following cities:

Algiers	Colombo	Lima	New York	Singapore
Athens	Copenhagen	Lisbon	Noumea	Stockholm
Auckland	Dhaka	London	Osaka	Suva
Baghdad	Dubai	Los An-	Paris	Teheran
Bangkok	Frankfurt	geles	Port Moresby	Tel Aviv
Beijing	Hamburg	Madrid	Rangoon	The Hague
Belgrade	Hanoi	Manila	Rio de	Tokyo
Berne	Hong Kong	Mauritius	Janeiro	Toronto
Bombay	Honolulu	Mexico City	Riyadh	Vancouver
Brussels	Houston	Miami	Rome	Vienna
Buenos Aires	Jakarta	Milan	San Francisco	Warsaw
Cairo	Jeddah	Moscow	Santiago	Washington
Caracas	Kuala	Nairobi	Seoul	Wellington
Chicago	Lumpur	New Delhi	Shanghai	

For information on the BMP contact on the of the Australian State offices:

NEW SOUTH WALES
R. J. (Bob) Salt—Senior Development Officer (Business
    Migration)
Department of State Development
Ground Floor, 139 Macquarie Street
Sydney NSW 2000
Tel: (02) 250 6666

Ken Carton—Director of Marketing
Albury–Wodonga Development Corporation
Ellis Street
Thurgoona NSW 2640
Tel: (060) 23 8000

VICTORIA
Bernie Delaney—Director, Business Migration
Department of Industry, Technology and Resources
228 Victoria Parade
East Melbourne VIC 3000
Tel: (03) 412 8000

WESTERN AUSTRALIA
Lesley Maher—Director, Business Migration Investment
    Services
The Western Australian Exim Corporation Ltd
10th Floor, London House
214 St George's Terrace
Perth WA 6000
Tel: (09) 481 0366

QUEENSLAND
Brian Hampton—Manager, Business Migration
Department of Industry Development
Enterprise House, 46 Charlotte Street
(GPO Box 1141)
Brisbane QLD 4001
Tel: (07) 224 8568

AUSTRALIAN CAPITAL TERRITORY
Alan Frazer—Manager, Projects and Business Migration
Canberra Development Board
PO Box 937
Civic Square
Canberra ACT 2608
Tel: (062) 75 8304

Australia's Location

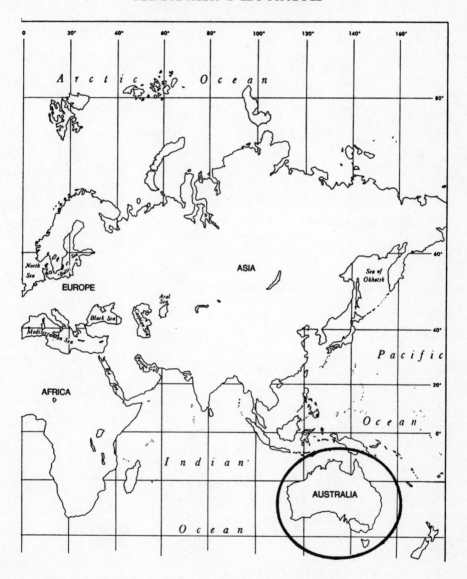

Chapter Two
Argentina: Options for Everyone

The Country and People

The Argentine Republic, situated in the south end of south America, occupies an area of 3,700,000 square kilometers, of which 2,791,810 square kilometers correspond to continental land and over 900,000 square kilometers to the Argentine sector on the Antarctic continent.

The country lies in the Southern Hemisphere, south of Paraguay and Bolivia, west of Chile, and west of Brazil.

Population figures record over 30,000,000 inhabitants, with density figures ranging from 14,000 persons per square kilometer in the city of Buenos Aires, down to 0.5 persons per square kilometer in the province of Santa Cruz in the southernmost area of Patagonia.

At present, 93% of the population consists of native citizens, most of which are descendants of immigrants from European countries, and 7% of foreign residents.

The great majority of the population is white. There are some interesting minority groups with their own cultural characteristics, such as native communities.

The official language is Spanish. There are other languages frequently used in the communities, such as Italian, French and English.

A large percentage of the Argentine population is Roman Catholic, but there are also large groups consisting of other religions such as Protestant, Greek Orthodox, and Jewish.

In spite of its extended dimension and its intense agricultural life, Argentina has very high figures of urban population (86%). Some towns hold over a million dwellers, and Buenos Aires, the federal capital, with its metropolitan area has 9,900,000 inhabitants. These urban centers concentrate the most appreciated and active cultural life, while in the rural areas life has preserved its traditions, which in some cases, dates back to pre-Columbian times.

To achieve permanent residency in Argentina you can invest in one of the many fields designated by the government. Included on the list are manufacturing, agriculture, breeding, mining, or fisheries. These are important to the economic development of the country which is struggling to overcome its enormous debt burden, runaway inflation, and its emergence into a new democratic order after years of military rule and oppression.

The size of the investment varies by geographical zones and the farthest away from the capital city of Buenos Aires the less the investment required. In general, investments begin in the area of $50,000 in outlying areas such as the four remote zones which are called "promotional areas" and up to $200,000 minimum in the capital.

Currency: Argentinian currency is the Austral. As of February, 1990 the foreign exchange rate for the volatile Argentinian currency was 1850 (Austral) equal to a U.S. Dollar.

Citizenship is issued after 2 years of permanent residency. (The application for citizenship may be filed after a year and a half of the permanent residency period.)

Overall, obtaining an Argentinean passport is very possible and special consideration should be given. The new democracy bodes well for economic recovery and potential. High standards of living exist in Argentina with an abundant supply of skilled labor. There is an European influence felt in the country, especially in the urban centers. Buenos Aires has always had the well deserved moniker as the "Paris of South America."

For more information contact any Argentinean Embassy or consulate or

Argentine Immigration Authorities
Dirección Nacional de Migraciones
Av. Antartica 1355,
1104 Buenos Aires, Argentina
Tel: 541-312-3288

Argentina's Location

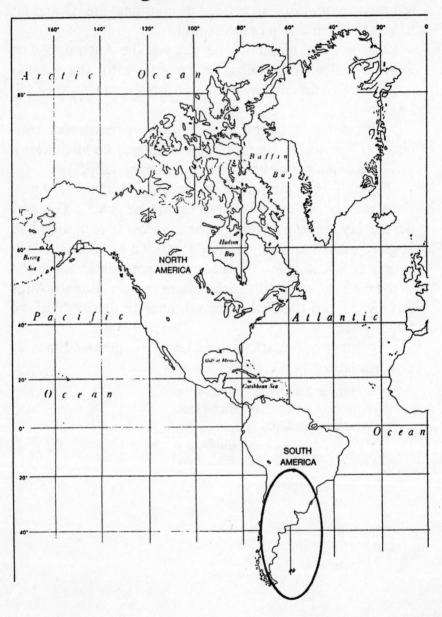

Chapter Three
Belgium: Major Asset

General Information About the Country and People

With its 11,779 square miles of territory, Belgium is approximately the size of the American state of Maryland—or the Japanese Kano Plain.

- Situated north of France, south of the Netherlands, with West Germany on the east, and Great Britain to the West
- Languages used in Belgium are Dutch (Flemish), French, and in certain cases German. English is frequently understood and spoken fluently
- Belgium has a population of 10.4 million
- Capital city: Brussels

- Belgium lies at the very heart of Western Europe, which makes it a choice potential location for a multinational company
- With a radius of 350 KM (220 miles) from Brussels there is a population of 200 million with a high standard of living. Within a radius of 350 km (220 miles) can be found the important centers of Amsterdam, Rotterdam, Frankfurt Dusseldorf, Paris, and Lille, and London. All of these cities can be reached within one hour flying time

Currency: As of February, 1990 the foreign exchange rate for the Belgian Frank was 35.155 Franks to one U.S. Dollar.

All the member states of the European Communities are busily preparing themselves for the incoming single market. This great transition is due to be completed by December 31, 1992 when all barriers to the free movement of people, goods, services, and capital will be removed. A massive undertaking, it will result in a single, integrated market of more than 320 million people.

Belgium is famous for its hospitality, which is also extended to foreign investors, who are attracted in particular by the favorable terms governing the setting up of companies in Belgium. These foreign businesses make a significant contribution to the country's economic prosperity, as moreover, do the 1,200 international organizations which have set up their headquarters in Belgium. Following recent measures, various foreign firms have set up their European center in Belgium.

Today, Belgium has the heaviest concentration of foreign investors on earth. There has got to be a reason why. In fact, there are many. Just for the record, Belgium exports account for 66% of the gross national product! This is on of the largest percentages among industrialized countries.

About Belgian Citizenship

In 1985 changes occurred in Belgian citizenship requirements which paved the way for new options for the potential investor. To achieve permanent residency status you are required to invest in the Belgian economy. The amount is variable and each application is dealt with on an individual basis. Belgium still has no official immigration policy but it does encourage investment and development of localized industry.

Belgian rules state that a 5 year residence is required for citizenship and the sought after passport. The bottom line is that the size of the investment. Rumors have it that the passport is quickly issued after the investment is "planted," even without residing in the country—a sharp contrast to the conditions prior to 1985. There are no immediate changes in Belgian immigration rules foreseen but there is a chance that a more welcome and open approach to entrepreneurs with fewer bucks to "plant" will be forthcoming.

Some Useful Addresses

Flanders Investment Opportunities Council (FIOC)
100 Trierstraat, 2nd Floor
1040 Brussels
Belgium
Tel: 32-2-2301225
Telex: 62073
Fax: 32-2-2309834

Belgian Banker's Association
rue Ravenstein 36
B-1000 Brussels
Tel: (2) 512 5868
Telex: 35575

Belgian National Federation of Chambers of Commerce and
    Industry
rue du Congrès 40
B-1000 Brussels
Tel: (2) 217 36 71

Federation of Belgian Chambers of Commerce Abroad
rue des Sols 8
B-1000 Brussels
Tel: (2) 512 26 33

Ministère des Affaires Economiques
Services des Investissements Etrangers
Square de Meeus 23
B-1040 Brussels
Tel: (2) 511 19 30
Telex: 61 932
Fax: (2) 514 03 89

For further particulars ...

Belgian Foreign Trade Office (BDBH/OBCE)
boulevard Emile Jacqmain 162, bte 36
B-1210 Brussels
Tel: (2) 219 44 50
Telex: 21 502
Fax: (2) 217 61 23

Chambre de Commerce du Grand-Duché de Luxembourg
rue Alcide de Gasperi 7
L-2981 Luxembourg
Tel: 43 59 53
Telex: 60 174
Fax: 43 83 26

Belgium's Location

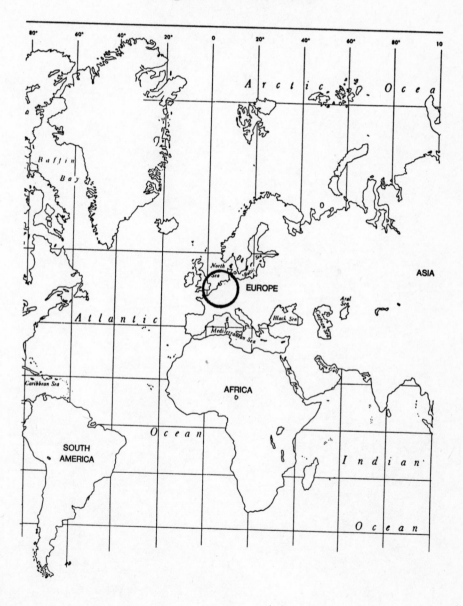

Chapter Four
Britain: The Bank's Assistance Makes the Difference

Britain is regarded as the pillar of culture, economy and finance in the western world, so we do not need to elaborate on information which every business person knows and which the British embassies throughout the world happily provides. We shall explain the basics of the domestic economy and we will touch on the central issue of citizenship which leads to a passport. Like other Common Market countries Britain is counting down to 1992 when Europe will become a single market consisting of approximately 320 million people.

London will strengthen its position as a financial leader and center in important economic fields after 1992 and would, in all likelihood become the capital of a united Europe.

Brief Points About the Economy

- Inflation—Reduced in the last few years to an average of 3%
- Employment—Since 1983 there has been an increase of more than 1.5. million in the labor force. This increase is greater than the rest of the E.E.C. combines
- Profits and profitability—Both of these have improved substantially in recent years. For example, the profits of industrial and commercial companies (non-North Sea) have grown rapidly since 1981, and profitability increased to 9% in 1986, the highest level since 1973
- Investment—Business investment, too, has reflected the buoyancy in the economy. It was 47% higher in 1987 than in 1981. A recent Investment Intentions Survey suggests further strong growth in the early 1990's

Setting up or expanding in Britain is fairly straightforward. The government actively supports foreign investment that will increase the total resources of the United Kingdom and improve its technical and managerial capabilities. To this end, it does not discriminate against overseas companies, does not constrain such activities as repatriation of profits, nor does it limit borrowing.

The Invest in Britain Bureau (IBB), part of the U.K's Department of Trade and Industry, is the primary government agency for foreign investment.

The Bureau operates overseas trough British embassies, high commissions, and consulates-general.

Citizenship and a Passport—
With the Bank's Assistance

A short cut to a British passport could be taken if a deposit is made of 150,000 British Pounds in a British bank. Citizenship status in the United Kingdom is a fixed $5\frac{1}{2}$ years and there are no exemptions for foreign investments. So this method of depositing 150,000 Pounds in a bank is a legitimate means of gaining citizenship. A depositor is free to do anything with the money as long as taxes are paid on profits. After receiving a passport, money can be transferred to any other country.

The bank branch guides the depositor/investor to a passport without requiring a long stay long or broken periods of residence in the U.K. The British banks publish in foreign papers the interest rates they give on foreign deposits. The terms offered are generally better than most other countries but it is advisable to check on the differences between banks.

In order to obtain more information about acquiring British citizenship and passport it is recommended to contact one of the many law firms that specialize in this process. Some of these firms are listed in this guide. In any case the short cut in the U.K. does not shorten the time needed.

An important advantage to those who hold a British passport is easy access to all countries that comprise the British Commonwealth and which were part of the British empire.

Currency: The value of the British Pound as of February 1990 was: 1.7 U.S. Dollars for one British Pound.

Addresses and Information

Invest in Britain Bureau

USA

New York

> Invest in Britain Bureau British Consulate General
> 11th Floor, 845 Third Avenue
> New York, NY 10022
> Tel: 212 593-2258
> Telex: 12-6208 (A/B PBDM NY)
> Fax: 212 421-7166 Ex 456
> Contact: John Rhodes, Jim Morrison, Nick McInnes, Libby
>   Bassett

Los Angeles

> British Consulate General
> Ahmanson Center
> 3701 Wilshire Boulevard
> Los Angeles, California 90010
> Tel: 213 385-7381
> Telex: 67-7421 (A/B BRITAIN LSA)
> Fax: 213 381-5450
> Contact: Bryan Davis, Barbara Cox

London

> Invest in Britain Bureau
> Department of Trade and Industry
> Kingsgate House
> 66-74 Victoria Street
> London SW1E 6SW
> Tel: 01-215 2541/2538
> Telex: 936069 DTIKH G
> Fax: 01-215 8451/01-931 0397
> Contact: Ray Burleigh

Montreal

British Consulate General
1155 University St.
Montreal H3B 3A7
Tel: 514 866-5863
Telex: 05561224 (A/B BRITAIN MTL)
Fax: 514 866-0202
Contact: Peter Newton

Toronto

British Consulate General, Suite 1910
College Park, 777 Bay Street
Toronto M5G 2G2
Tel: 416 593-1290
Telex: 06524486 (A/B BRITAIN TOR)
Fax: 416 593-1229
Contact: Bryan Sparrow

To obtain more information that is not available through the "official channels," please write to:

David Garrick & Co
39 Queen Anne St.
London WIM 9FA

Britain's Location

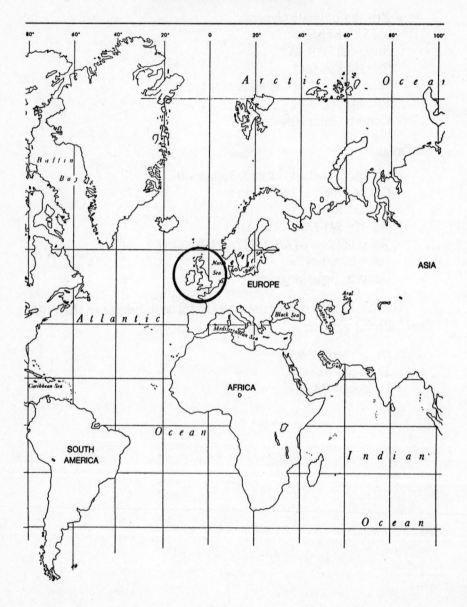

Chapter Five
Canada: The Country with Unlimited Opportunities

General Information About the Country

Canada is the world's second largest country, occupying most of the northern half of North America. Its 4,000 mile border with the United States is the world's longest undefended international boundary. Canada is divided into 10 provinces and two territories.

The present population is over 25 million, with more than half living in the highly industrialized area in Southern Ontario and Quebec, close to the main population centers in the Northeastern part of the United States. Montreal and Toronto each have over 3 million residents; other principle cities include Vancouver, Calgary, Edmonton, Winnipeg, Windsor, London, Hamilton, Ottawa (the national capital), Quebec, Saint John, and Halifax.

Both English and French are official languages. French predominates in the Province of Quebec, where it is the official language. English is used consistently throughout most of the rest of the country. In addition, as a result of recent immigration, various other languages are often used in local communities.

Currency: The monetary unit is the Canadian Dollar ($; international symbol, CDN), consisting of 100 cents. Once pegged to the U.S. Dollar, the Canadian Dollar has been allowed to float in recent years in relation to other world currencies.

1. Foreign exchange and repatriation of profits

Canada has no foreign exchange controls or currency restrictions on the ownership, export or import of precious metals used for trading or investment purposes.

2. The Canadian dollar is fully convertible

As of February, 1990 the value of one Canadian Dollar was 0.84 of one U.S. Dollar.

Economic and Social Indicators

Based on the Gross National Product (GNP) Canada's economy ranks sixth among the 24 member countries of the Organization for Economic Cooperation Development. It is preceded by the U.S., France, Germany, Italy and Japan.

The Gross Domestic Product (GDP) is a measure of production originating from within Canada regardless of whether factors of production are Canadian or non-resident. GDP increased by 8.6% IN 1987 to $554 million. A brief review of the distribution of GDP in 1987 indicates that the majority value of the GNP originated from the service industry. The breakdown between the various factors is as follows:

Service Producing Sector

Community, business and personal services	19.9%
Government services	6.2%
Finance, insurance and real estate	14.3%
Wholesale and retail trade	12.1%
Transportation, storage and communication	7.7%
Total in 1987	60.3%

Goods Producing Sector

Electric power, gas and water utilities	3.1%
Construction	7.1%
Manufacturing	19.7%
Mines, quarries and oil wells	5.8%
Agriculture, Forestry, fishing and trapping	4.0%
Total in 1987	39.7%

Serving as a land-bridge between Europe and the Far East, Canada stands at the northern edge of the lucrative North American market.

The United States is by far Canada's most important trading partner, receiving about 65% of Canada's export.

Canada–United States Free Trade Agreement

Canada has negotiated a landmark trade agreement with the United States to liberalize trade between the two countries. The Free Trade Agreement, which has not yet been ratified, will probably bring about major changes in Canadian business. The agreement aims to eliminate tariffs and any remaining import restrictions on trade within 10 years. It seeks to give Canadian businesses assures access to a combined market of 275 million people and create for Canada substantial overall gains in employment, real wages investment production, and lower prices. The benefits and risks are not yet well defined, an extensive debit sand discussions are still continuing as the ratification process proceeds. Canada's industrial activity has been, and continues to be significantly influenced by the economy of the United States, its closest neighbor and trading partner. In 1986 about $3 billion or 44%, of foreign direct investment came from the United States.

The multicultural nature of the Canadian society also fosters international integration of the country's business community. Canada is a home to people with a diverse ethnic background who have maintained social and economic ties with relatives and associates abroad. Approximately 11% of the Canadian population claims a first language other than English or French. Metropolitan Toronto contains one of the largest Italian populations outside of Italy. Canada's Prairie provinces have substantial Ukrainian and German communities. And British Columbia has a growing Chinese population.

Canada's multicultural research serve international economic integration in two ways. Foreign business people may find it easier to establish a foothold in the country through Canadians of similar ethnic backgrounds. And Canadian businesses expending their operation abroad can take into the country's multicultural resources for linguistic expertise as well as familiarity with overseas markets and business practice. In recent years Canada has experienced strong immigration from Asia and the Middle East, which has further enhanced Canada's ethnic diversity and strengthened important social and business ties with the fast growing economies of these regions.

Immigration and the Passport

Immigration to Canada is the Federal responsibility. Canada encourages visitors for a variety of reasons, including the fostering of trade and commerce. Canada's immigration policy would probably be described as relatively open-door, however admission is generally dependent on prospective employment opportunity which can not be filled by a current resident or by a resident who could be trained to fill the position. Generally, though, non residents intending to acquire or to start up a business in Canada that will create employment opportunities for Canadian residents stand high in priority preference as immigrants. Canadian citizenship may be applied for after residing in Canada for three years and subsequently be entitled to a passport.

Basic qualifications

Canada has a business immigration program to attract

business people who will create jobs and contribute to the economic development. There are three categories of business immigrants—entrepreneurs, investor, and self-employed persons.

The entrepreneur

These immigrants are experienced business people who wish to buy or start a business in which they will have an active managerial role. The business must create jobs for one or more Canadians and must and make a significant contribu- tion to the economy. This category includes business peo- ple who are experienced in managing small-to medium sized enterprises.

The investor

Prospective investor immigrants must have a proven busi- ness record and have accumulated through their own en- deavors, a personal net worth of at least $500,000 (Cana- dian). They must invest as required in one of the investment tiers described below.

Under tier one, qualified investors may be eligible if they have a net worth of $500,000 and make an investment of $150,000 locked in for three years, in a province which, in the previous year, has received fewer than three per cent of Canada's business immigrants.

Under tier two, qualified investors may be eligible if they have a net worth of $500,000 and make an investment of $250,000 locked in for three yeas.

Under tier three qualified investors may be eligible if they have a net worth of $700,000 and make an investment of $500,000 locked in for five years.

The self-employed

These immigrants will establish will establish a business in Canada that employs only themselves. The business must contribute to the economy, of the cultural or artistic life of Canada. This category includes farmers, sport personalities, artists, members of the performing arts, and owners of small community businesses.

Canadian immigration, as far as we know, does not insist on continual residency during the three year residency period for acquiring citizenship and subsequently a passport. As a business person you are entitled to leave Canada for a period of under 183 days per year, to attend to "other" business dealings. This "bend-over-backwards" policy of accommodating investors should easily accommodate all those who need flexibility and convenience. We stress that a Canadian passport is on the same standard as the Australian one and is considered in the top scale of practical and reputable passports. They also allow you to enter most of the countries in the world.

Useful Contacts and Addresses

Canadian Government Contacts

Industry, Science and Technology Canada
235 Queen Street
Ottawa, Ontario K1A 0H5
CANADA
Tel: (613) 995-5771
Telex: 053-4123
Facsimile: (613) 954-1894

Investment Canada
P.O. Box 2800, Station D
Ottawa, Ontario K1P 6A5
CANADA
Tel: (613) 995-0465
Telex: 053-4450
Facsimile: (613) 996-2515

Federal Business Development Bank
P.O. Box 335
800 Victoria Square
Montreal, Quebec H4Z 1L4
Tel: (514) 283-5904
Telex: 055-60707
Facsimile: (514) 283-0617

Export Development Corporation
P.O. Box 655
Ottawa, Ontario K1P 5T9
CANADA
Tel: (613) 598-2500
Cable: XCREDCORP
Telex: 053-4136
Facsimile: (613) 237-2690

Atlantic Canada Opportunities Agency
P.O. Box 6051
770 Main Street, 10th Floor
Moncton, New Brunswick 31C 9J8
CANADA
Tel: 1-800-561-7862 (toll free)

External Affairs Canada (EAC)
Head Office
Lester B. Pearson Bldg.
125 Sussex Drive
Ottawa, Ontario K1A 0G2
Tel: 1-800-267-8376

Employing and Immigration Canda (EIC)
Head Office
Place du Portage, Phase IV
140 Promenade du Portage
Hull, Quebec K1A 0J9
Tel: (819) 994-2949
(Communications Centre)

Employment and Immigration Canada
Ottawa, Ontario K1A 0J9
CANADA
Tel: (819) 994-7141

And, for more information, contact your nearest Canadian Embassies/Consulates/High Commissions:

United States: Atlanta, Boston, Buffalo, Chicago, Cleveland, Dallas, Detroit, Los Angeles, Minneapolis, New York, Orlando, Philadelphia, San Francisco, Santa Clara, Seattle, Washington, D.C.

Europe: Brussels, Copenhagen, The Hague, Helsinki, Oslo, Madrid, Stockholm, Berne, London, Bonn, Dusseldorf, Paris, Rome, Milan, Munich, Vienna

Middle East: Riyadh, Tel Aviv, Kuwait, Cairo

Pacific Rim: Tokyo, Osaka, Hong Kong, Beijing, Canberra, Sydney, Wellington, Seoul, Singapore

Canada's Location

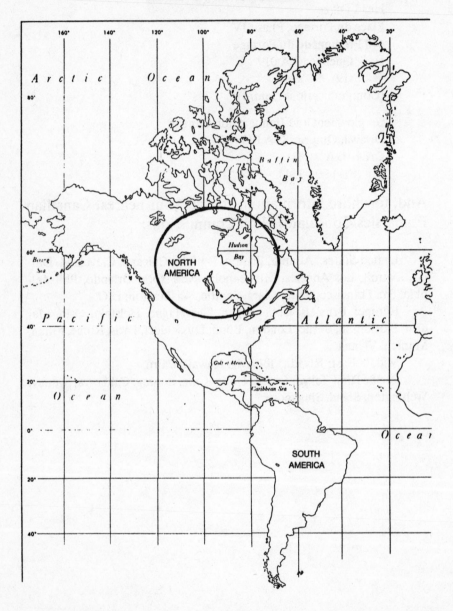

Chapter Six
Chile: South America's Park by the Seashore

General Information About the Country

Spanish army captains Diego de Almagro in 1536 and Pedro de Valdivia in 1540 opened the country to Spanish colonization and domination which was to last over three centuries. Santiago, the capital city, was founded in 1541.

Chile is the southernmost country in South America, bordering the Pacific Ocean. Its neighbors are Bolivia to the Northeast, Peru to the North, and Argentina to the East.

With a population of approximately 13,000,000 inhabitants, with the majority concentrated in and around the capital city of Santiago in the central zone, this Spanish speaking country is ethnically composed of various indigenous groups who arrived at different times. Each has developed its own culture independently, and has given Chile a multi-faceted culture.

Chilean Industry

Chile has developed important industrial activity from the processing of its own raw materials either of mining (oil refining, iron foundry, copper manufacture), forest (paper, pulp, and sawn wood), marine (fish meal, fish oil, frozen and canned fish), or farming origin (dairy plants, agroindustry, sugar beet plants). There are likewise important industries using mainly imported raw materials or incorporating foreign-origin parts and pieces. These are the cases of the textile, shoe leather, milling, automobile assembling, machinery-workshop, home appliance and pharmaceutical industry and others.

Economic and Social Indicators

Growth Rate of Gross Geographical Product: 1988: 6.8 per cent
Total Exports: (millions FOB U.S. Dollars) 1988: 7,051.8.
Total Imports: (millions FOB U.S. Dollars) 1988: 4,833.2
Trade Balance: (millions U.S. Dollars) 1988: 2,218.6
Current Account: (millions U.S. Dollars) 1986: 1,137; 1987: 811; 1988: 167.4
Balance of Payments: (millions U.S. Dollars) 1988: 731.8.
Inflation: 1988 12.7 per cent

Exchange Rate: As of February, 1990 the foreign exchange rate for the volatile Chilean currency was 286 Chile Pesos equal to 1 U.S. Dollar.

Monthly Chilean Labor Cost, June 1988

Labor Ranking	Chilean Pesos	U.S. Dollars
General Manager	770,000	3,420
Assistant Manager	615,000	2,740
Chief Accountant	355,000	1,580
Head of Plant	425,000	1,900
Head of Shifts	120,000	530
Workers	36,000	160
Chief Lawyer	330,000	1,480
Secretary to the Management	48,000	210
Telephone Operator	40,000	180
Driver	48,000	210
Messenger-boy	36,000	160

Becoming an Investor in Chile

It is necessary to file applications with the Foreign Investment Committee's Executive Secretariat indicating all particulars and general information about the proposed project. After the application is approved the foreign investor and the Chilean government enter into a foreign investment contract by means of a public deed.

A contract is drawn up according to a standard model drafted by the Executive Secretariat and must be signed before six months have elapsed since its authorization. The contract establishes the investor's warranties and rights such as capital profit remittance, access to the exchange market, taxation treatment, etc.

The foreign investment policy in Chile is based on three fundamental principles: equal treatment for national and foreign investors alike; free access to the various markets and economic segments, and the State's minimum interference in regard to their activity.

We briefly reviewed the characteristics natural conditions and the typical industrial situation in Chile. We stress, after advice from the Chilean Commercial Consul in New York that upon investment of a minimum sum of $25,000 in almost any field of business; a small store, for example, small industrial factory, or even a brokerage office, an investor and family are entitled to permanent residency within as little as a month!

The local residency regulations state that after five years of permanent residency one is entitled to citizenship and a passport. There are no restrictions, as in Australia, for example, on having to stay continuously within the country's borders. The terms, in fact, are so flexible, that if the investor preferred living outside Chile all that need be done is to contact a Chilean Embassy or Consulate once a year (maximum four times) to fill out proper forms. The only actual time that need be spent in Chile is a cumulative of one year!

Useful Information and Addresses

For more information about investment opportunities in Chile contact:

International Economic Relations Secretariat (PROCHILE)
Pedro De Valdivia 0193 (Head Office)
Santiago, Chile
Tel: 231-71-08

or outside of Chile you can obtain information from Chilean embassies and consulates.

North America

Embassy in Canada: 56 Sparks St., suite 801, Ottawa.

General Consulates: 1010 St. Catherine West, suite 731, Montreal; 220 Bay St., suite 1003, Toronto; 1124 Lansdale Ave., suite 305, North Vancouver.

Embassy in the United States: 1732 Mass. Ave., N.W., Washington, DC.

General Consulates: 866 United Nations Plaza, room 302, N.Y.; 510 6th St., suite 1204, Los Angeles; 25 SE Second Ave., suite 801, Ingraham Bldg., Miami; 600 Travis St., suite 3825, Houston; 870 Market St., room 1062, San Francisco; 333 North Michigan Ave., suite 728, Chicago.

Europe

German Federal Republic Embassy: Kronprinzinstrasse 20, 5300 Bonn 2.

General Consulates: Havestehuder Weg 7, 2000 Hamburg 13; Bundesplatz 12, 1000 Berlin 31; Humboldtstrasse 94, 6000 Frankfurt am Main; Mariannestrasse 5, 8000 München 22.

Embassy in Austria: Vienna 1010 Lugeck 1 3 9 Vienna.

Embassy in Belgium: avenue Luise 251, 1050 Bruxelles.

Embassy in Denmark: Kastelsvej 15, 3rd floor, 2100 Copenhagen DK.

Embassy in Spain: Lagasca 88, 60 piso, Madrid 1.

General Consulate: Gran Via de las Cortes Catalanas 591, 30 piso, 08007 Barcelona.

Embassy in France: 2 avenue De la Motte-Picquet, 75007 Paris.

General Consulate: Bâtiment G, "Le Ribera," avenue Prado 376, 13008 Marseille.

Embassy in Italy: Via Nazionale No. 54, 20 piso int, 4 e 5, Roma.

General Consulate: Via di Santa Zita No. 1, Interno 7, Genoa.

Embassy in Norway: Meltzers Gate 5, Oslo 2.

Embassy in Holland: Mauritskade 51, 2514 HG, The Hague.

Embassy in the United Kingdom: 12, Devonshire St., London W1N 2 DS.

General Consulate: 11th Floor, Hua Hsia Bldg., 64 Gloucester Road, Hong Kong.

Embassy in Rumania: Bulevard Ana Ipatescum 8, Bucharest.

Embassy: The Vatican: Piazza Risorgimento 55, Interno 19 20 00192, Roma.

Embassy in Sweden: Kommindorsgatan 35, 5th floor, 114 58, Stockholm.

Embassy in Switzerland: Eigerplatz 5, 12 floor, 3007 Bern.

General Consulate: Dufourstrasse 101, 8008 Zurich.

General Consulate in Yugoslavia: Vasiliyagacese 9-A, 11040 Belgrade.

Africa

Embassy at Arab Republic of Egypt: 5, Shagaret El Dorr Zamalec, Cairo.

Ivory Coast: Boite Postale 1367, Abidjan 08.

Gabon: B.P. 736, Libreville.

Embassy in Kenya: International Life House 5th Floor, Mama Ngina St., P.O. Box 45554, Nairobi.

Embassy in Morocco: 141 route des Zaers, Rabat.

Republic of South Africa: Merino Building 7th floor, P.O. Box 2073, Pretoria.

General Consulate: Heeringracht Tower, Cape Town Centre Building, 7th floor, suite 712, Cape Town.

Zaire: 45 avenues des Trois "Z," Bldg. Mozart, Zne de la Gombe P.O. Box 15892, KIN 1, Kinshasa.

Asia

People's Republic of China: San Li Tun Dong Si Jie No. 1, Peking.

South Korea: 142-5 Itaewon Dong Yongsan-Ku, Seoul.

Embassy in Philippines: 2nd Floor A, Gammon Centre Bldg., 126 Alfaro St., Salcedo Village, Makati Metro, Manila.

Embassy in India: 113 Shantiniketan 110021, New Delhi.

Embassy in Indonesia: Gedung Arthaloka Lantai 14, Jalan Jindral Sudirman NO.2, P.O. Box 4615, Djakarta.

Embassy in Israel: Pinkas 54, Dpto. 45, 11th Floor, Tel Aviv 62261, P.O. Box 21278.

Embassy in Japan: Nihon Seimei Akabanebashi Bldg. 8th Floor 1-4, Shiba 3-Chome, Minato-Ku, Tokyo.

Embassy in Jordan: Ibn Hani St., Shmeisani Amman, P.O. Box 1845, Amman.

Embassy in Lebanon: Inmueble Iranien, 2ème étage, Elyssar, Route de Bikfaya, Beirut.

Embassy in Pakistan: House 10, Street 62, F6-3.

Embassy in Singapur: 16 Raffles Quay 43-03, floor 43 Hong Leong Bldg. Singapore 0106.

Embassy in Syria: Charkasieh-Chaura, Damascas.

Embassy in Thailand: 15, Sukhumvit Road, S01 61, Klongton, Bangkok.

Embassy in Turkey: Cinnah Caddesi 78 1 Cankaya, Ankara.

Oceania

Embassy in Australia: 93 Endeavour St. Red Hill, Canberra Act 2603, P.O. Box 69, Monard Crescent, Canberra.

General Consulates: Suite 2004, 20th Floor, 338 George St., Sidney; 459 Collins Street, Floor 14, City Mutual Bldg., P.O. Box 1674N, Melbourne.

Embassy in New Zealand: Robert Jones House, 12th Floor, Jervois Quay, Wellington.

In the majority of our embassies and general consulates, it is possible to obtain detailed tourist information published by SERNATUR, the National Tourist Board.

Chile's Location

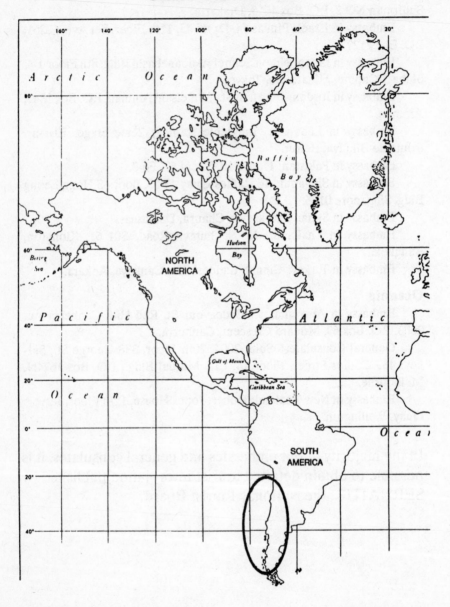

Chapter Seven
Dominican Republic: Tourism Industry Bonanza

General Information About the Country and People

Geography

The second largest nation in the Caribbean, covering 18,700 square miles. Occupies two thirds of the island of Hispaniola (Haiti occupies the western one third). Population is 6.5 million (1987 estimate), with a labor force of 2 million (27% unemployment).

History

Christopher Columbus encountered Hispaniola in 1492. The Dominican Republic has been an independent nation since 1844. General. Rafael Trujillo Molina overthrew an elected government in 1930 and ruled until 1961, when he was assassinated. After a period of instability, a civil war that broke out in 1965 was ended with the intervention of the U.S. military. Since 1966, there have been democratic elections every four years, with power shifting between major key political parties: the Reformist Party, and the Dominican Revolutionary Party.

Official language

Spanish, with English widely spoken by business and government leaders.

Foreign trade

Exports in 1987 were valued at about U.S.$750 million, with shipments to the United States worth approximately U.S.$560 million. Key exports were: sugar, coffee, gold, furniture, apparel. Imports in 1987 were about U.S.$1.35 billion including U.S.$560 million from the U.S., mainly foodstuffs, textiles, machinery, and chemicals.

Key incentives for investors

Currency: As of February, 1990 one American dollar is equal to 6.28 Dominican Pesos.

The Dominican Republic offers a large, productive workforce. The legal minimum wage is RD $350 per month (about U.S. $70). Special tax incentives are available to investors in free zones, tourism and agriculture. The country enjoys political stability, has a good infrastructure, and is easily accessible from major U.S. cities. Under the Caribbean Basin Economic Recovery Act, approved by Washington and in effect since 1984, a number of products enter the U.S. duty free.

178 companies in the "free zone"

The Dominican Republic is burdened by a substantial foreign debt. Most of its 6.5. million people are poor, but eager for a better life.

In the past two years, their hopes have been buoyed by an exceptional surge in new investment, not only in manufacturing, but also in tourism and agribusiness. the combination of new public and private sector investment fueled a startling economic growth rate of 11% in 1987, raising concerns about inflation.

At last count (and the number keeps rising quite swiftly) some 178 firms from the U.S., Europe, and the Far East have located in the nation's nine industrial free zones, according to Arelis Rodriguez, executive director of the investment promotion Council of the Dominican Republic.

Tenants in the free zones manufacture apparel, textiles, electrical components, jewelry, cigars, leather articles, fur coats, pharmaceuticals and a wide range of other products. There is also a vigorous growth in such "high tech" areas as data processing and computer graphics.

"Employment in the free zones has reached 70,000, compared with 20,000 as recently as 1974," says Ms. Rodriguez.

Foreign investors are attracted to the free zones by a convenient, sheltered environment, free of taxes (for 12 to 20 years) and import duties, with unrestricted repatriation of profits. They are also attracted by the country's political stability, modern infrastructure, proximity to the U.S. by air and sea, and a low-cost workforce of two million people

Government Policy Towards Attracting Investments

"The Government of the Dominican Republic is dedicated to promote the best possible conditions for private investment, both national and foreign," says President Joaquin Balaguer, the 80 year old leader who was elected to a fifth term in 1986, and is helping to spur the economy with a massive public works program designed to improve the nation's infrastructure.

"Last year," says President Balaguer, "some $80 million in foreign capital added vitality to our renewed economy. Our free zones, for example, offer extraordinary incentives to businesses of all sizes and types. Tourism is also emerging with great strength. And there is also considerable enthusiasm over non-traditional agriculture, as well as information services."

Tourism is perhaps the most buoyant sector of the economy; hundreds of millions of dollars are being invested in resort properties in the Dominican Republic, which is on its way to becoming the leading destination in the Caribbean.

Factory wages in the Dominican Republic, at current exchange rates, average about 60 cents an hours, including fringe benefits. Even at higher skill levels, wages are much lower than in the U.S., with experienced mechanics and electricians earning $310 a month, managers $880, and engineers, just under $1,100. A number of the free zone tenants are operating under "twin plant" arrangements, processing their products in both nearby Puerto Rico and the Dominican Republic. This enables them to qualify for exemption from corporate federal taxes under section 936 of the Internal Revenue Code.

It is important to point out that the Dominican Republic is under heavy American influence; politically, economically, and militarily. Americans have already heavily invested in local industry. Like other third world countries in the region the Dominican Republic opened a free zone to attract foreign investment.

Today the most advanced industry in the Dominican Republic is tourism. In tourism the Dominican Republic gives tax exemptions and other benefits. Other industries are not as well stimulated and encouraged and are not top priority for the government.

The size of the investment required is substantial, but is not risky and has high profit potential in tourism. The initial investment is recovered more rapidly than other fields. All of this is due to the real travel and recreational values offered in a tropical Caribbean island, and with advertising and promotion in the mass media in the U.S., Canada, and to a lesser degree, in Western Europe, tourism in the Dominican Republic is its number one industry.

The Dominican coordinator of foreign investments has informed us that citizenship and a passport could be issued, under certain circumstances in only a week's time! Obviously, the size of investment has the greatest influence. An "ordinary" investor must open up and provide job opportunities to at least 15 local inhabitants and direct its product mainly for exports. A permanent residency would be issued within a week or two and citizenship in a matter of a year or two. Unofficial sources inform us that if an investor has the right "connections" citizenship and a passport are obtainable in as little as 6 months.

Dominican officials are very helpful, as in Jamaica, towards an investment project, trying to insure success and keep a reputation for providing solid investment opportunities.

For additional information on investments in the Dominican Republic and means of obtaining citizenship you can write to embassies or consulate nearest you or to a law firm which specializes in investment as a means of obtaining citizenship.

Information and Addresses

For general information and assistance, contact Antonio Caceres Troncoso, President, or Arelis Rodriguez, Executive Director,

> Investment Promotion Council
> Av. Abraham Lincoln
> Edif. Alico, 2do piso
> Santo Domingo
> Dominican Republic
> Tel: 809-532-3281.86
> Fax: 809-533-7029

Ask to see their 12-minute videotape presentation that summarizes investment opportunities in the Dominican Republic. The IPC also has available informative brochures.

Also helpful is the 2,000-member

American Chamber of Commerce of the Dominican Republic
Hotel Santo Domingo
P.O. Box 95-2
Santo Domingo
Dominican Republic
Tel: 809-533-7292 or 533-7414

Write to Executive Vice President Wilson A. Rood and request the Chamber's comprehensive 344-page Investors Handbook, available postpaid for U.S.$20.

Kaplan Russin Vecchi & Iglesias
Paseo de la Castellana, 155-2 D
Madrid 28046
Spain
Tel: 270-7320/270-7741
Telex: 46780 KRUSE

Kaplan Russin Vecchi & Perenzin
Carrera 7, No. 17-51, Suite 709
Apartado Aereo 20986
Bogotá
Colombia
Tel: 243-7067-68/242-1811
Telex: 45347 KAPRU CO

Kaplan Russin Vecchi & Parker
Bank Tower, 9th Floor
205 Tun Hwa N. Road
Taipei
Taiwan, Republic of China
Tel: 712-8956
Telex: 23775 KAPRUS

Kaplan Russin & Vecchi
(International Legal Counsellors Thailand, Ltd.)
Bangkok Bank Building, 18th Floor
333 Silom Road
Bangkok 10500
Thailand
Tel: 236-0151/235-0780
Telex: 81166 LAWYERS TH 20486 LAWYERS TH

There are associated offices in Buenos Aires, Caracas, Guatemala City, Hong Kong, London, Manila, Quito, San Juan, Santiago, and Sydney.

Dominican Republic's Location

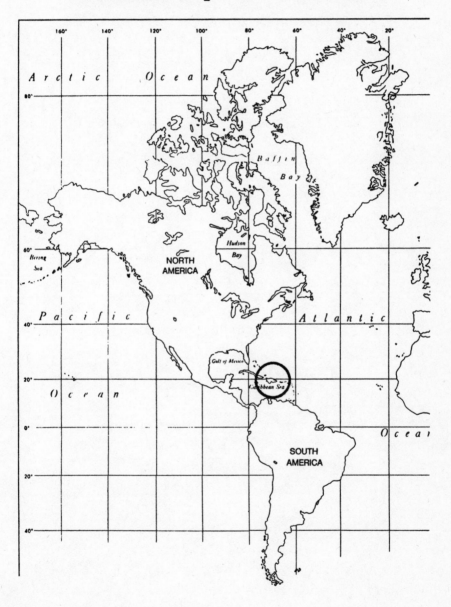

Chapter Eight
Guatemala: Entrepreneur's Playground

Introduction—Country and People

Guatemala covers an area of 108,889 square kilometers (42,042 square miles). Northernmost of the five Central American countries, Guatemala has the largest population with approximately 7.5 million inhabitants. It is bordered on the north and west by Mexico, on the South by the Pacific Ocean, and on the east by the Atlantic Ocean (Caribbean Sea). Honduras, and El Salvador. The country is divided into four regions; the two coastal areas, the highlands, and the Peten.

The major city and center of government and trade is Guatemala City, which has an estimated population of more than 1.5 million. The language of the country is Spanish, but the Indian population speaks at least 10 different dialects. Roman Catholicism is the predominant religion.

Over 50% of the population is under 18 years of age. About 35% of the population lives in the cities and the remaining people live in rural areas.

Guatemala is principally an agricultural country, where agriculture constitutes 25% of its Gross Domestic Product (GDP), employs close to 55% of its labor force, and represents over 60% of its exports.

The GDP, based on economic activity, is distributed as follows:

Activity	% of GDP
Agriculture	25
Commerce	26
Industry	16
Transport and Communications	7
Construction	3
Services and Other	23

The principal exports continue to be coffee, cardamom, and sugar, although other, non-traditional agricultural exports are increasing in importance. Guatemala has the potential of becoming an exporter of oil and other minerals.

The term investment has quite a flexible meaning in Guatemala. An investment can mean the renting of a farm on a monthly basis. Or it can mean opening a brokerage office of any kind in Guatemala City, for example. It sounds strange, but a brokerage of any sort will do—real estate, commodities, financial, or even "information." This takes a minor investment and many people, including financial tycoons have found this loophole and opened offices in Guatemala City. Foreign investors are not granted tax advantages and are considered as local business people who set up new industry. The initial investment is not reimbursable, but it may be as low as, perhaps, $1000 to open up a new business and an office. Small price to pay for a passport!?

On the down side there is a Guatemalan law which prohibits the granting of citizenship and a passport just on the grounds of investment. For this the usual routine steps must be taken in normally applying for citizenship: after being issued a temporary residency visa there is the application for temporary residency. Another 2 or 3 years lapse before application can be made for permanent residency status, and still another 3 or 4 years for citizenship. Investors benefit, however, by being allowed to apply for permanent residency after a year's stay. At the end of a five year period citizenship would be granted to those who had a continuous residency in Guatemala with the exception of absence permitted at not more than a year from Guatemala. If this condition can not be met the applicant must eventually prove a continuous residence in the country of five years within a ten year period.

There are exceptions to the rules, of course. The President of the country has the power to grant citizenship to outstanding individuals two years after residency. Those individuals, either academic scholars, artists, or people in business, who have helped in the development and progress of Guatemalan industry, culture or society. If the candidate is in business, investments must be made wisely to be considered for such citizenship out of "excellence." The sum need not be extremely large but must make some "ripples." In brokerage of know-how the investment is not usual large in any case, but the results can be very fruitful in business.

As in many countries in Latin and South America it is advisable, when opening a business, to make an association with a local business person. There are seemingly perpetual political problems in Guatemala which makes it prudent to hedge one's bets. If in the event of trouble, the local "partner" always will have a foothold in the business.

Another option regarding Guatemala is retirement there. (See chapter on "Passport as a Retirement Reward.")

For more information contact the Guatemalan embassies and consulates around the world. Another useful address is of the law firm of Klynveld, Peat, Marnick, and Goerdeler. They specialize in investments and obtaining passports. They have branches all over the world and one of the 250 offices should be in your local telephone directory.

Guatemala's Location

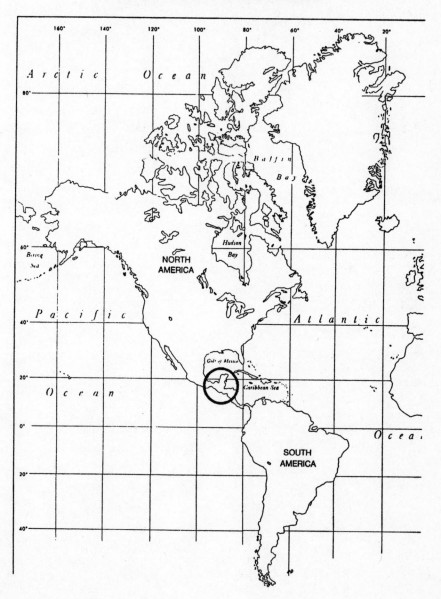

Chapter Nine
Jamaica: Growth
in the Caribbean

Introduction—Country and People

Jamaica was encountered by Columbus in 1494. Jamaica's
independence was attained from the British in August,
1962 and is now a parliamentary democracy within the
British Commonwealth. The Queen us represented by the
Governor General.

Location and size

Jamaica is approximately 550 miles Southeast of Miami and
less than 2,000 miles from New York City. Its capital is
Kingston.

    With an area of 4,244 square miles, Jamaica is the
third largest island in the Caribbean. It is a fertile land

of high mountains, tropical forests, magnificent beaches, and natural resources that include bauxite, gypsum, and limestone.

Population

2.3 million inhabitants live on the island. The population is diverse and largely of African descent, but with a mixture of Chinese, East Indian, and European ancestries. The nations's motto is "Out of Many, One People."

Unemployment is more than 40%. The Official language is English (most people also speak an English-based Creole). The literacy rate is 75% and life expectancy is 71 years. Infant mortality is 28 per thousand. Per capita income is $1,130 (1987 figure).

Currency: The country's currency is the Jamaican Dollar. As of February, 1990 the exchange rate was 6.95 Jamaican Dollars equal to one U.S. Dollar.

Jamaica's economy is undergoing a dramatic, sometimes painful, transition. From the 18th century through early in this century, it was based on the cultivation of sugar cane. Sugar has suffered a long period of decline, but is still the largest agricultural export of Jamaica and an important source of jobs.

Since its independence in 1962 Jamaica has been suffering from economic problems and is in dire need of foreign investments to nurture its growth. Jamaica is located in a problematic area for business, but it has exporting benefits to the United States. Currently, unemployment in Jamaica is running at over 40%; a danger to the stability of the government and the region.

In order to attract foreign investment in Jamaica, the government offers bait—citizenship in practically no time for those prepared to invest significantly.

In 1988 the government of Jamaica created JAMPRO, a new umbrella agency responsible for the nation's investment and trade promotion program. It incorporates JNIP and two other agencies: Jamaica National Export Corp. (JNEC), and Jamaica Industrial Development Corporation (JDIC).

JAMPRO has been successful in attracting new investments to Jamaica and, after apparel, significant investments have been made in agribusiness, tourism, and data entry services. Other priority areas being promoted by the JAMPRO are footwear, electronics, furniture (Jamaica has skilled crafts people who turn out excellent antique furniture reproductions), ceramics and glassware (Jamaica has quality raw materials for these products) and industrial minerals (there are large deposits of limestone, gypsum, marble, and a variety of clays).

Jamaica has also adopted a government-owned "free zone," which is quite common among third world nations. To lure investors, the government has created certain zones, usually in port areas, which allow for importation of goods tax free if they are to be used in the investor's Jamaican business venture for export only.

Investors are expected to establish or invest in industries which will export goods and provide jobs for local residents.

Just a few short years ago representatives of JAMPRO informed us that the minimum investment in Jamaica required to obtain a Jamaican passport was $100,000. In mid 1989 the minimum has been lowered to $40,000! We can safely assume that, in reality, the actual amount will be somewhere between $40,000 and $100,000. The investor must provide jobs for a minimum of 30 people, with 75% of the jobs going to local inhabitants. This demand does not encourage investment in high-tech progressive industry because local manpower is generally unskilled and untrained.

Statistically, it has been shown that most investments are recovered after 8–10 years. The financial institution that handles foreign investments is the Bank of Jamaica. The bank also is a source of information about Jamaican markets. Officials direct investors to specific opportunities and check each one out very thoroughly before allowing a business transaction to take place. The bank and the government remain very active in all investment transactions involving foreigners and this helps to provide a measure of safety in the investment. The government also does not want to lure bad business.

In addition to the investment sum, the government requires the same sum as collateral. This amount is deposited in the Bank of Jamaica to cover debts, should they arise. This collateral is returned as soon as the business can shown to be running and solvent.

Immediately after depositing the collateral the investor will receive a permanent residency document and a travel certificate, including spouse and children under 18. Permanent citizenship which earns a passport takes 3–5 years from the time of investment. According to local practice, a 5 year residency is "officially" required.

In Jamaica, unlike many other neighboring countries mentioned in this book, the government helps insure the success of the investor and the local business by becoming unofficial "partners" in the venture.

Where to Obtain More Information on Investment Opportunities in Jamaica

Jamaica

35 Trafalgar Road
Kingston Road
Kingston 5
Jamaica, W.I.
Tel: (809) 929-7190, 929-8217, 929-8235, 929-9450-61
Telex: 2222 JANIPRO
Fax: (809) 924-9650

Mutual Life Building
30 Market Street, 5th Floor
Montego Bay, St. James
Jamaica, W.I.
Tel: (809) 952-3420
Fax: (809) 952-1384

21 Ward Avenue
Mandeville, Manchester
Jamaica, W.I.
Tel: (809) 962-0734
Fax: (809) 962-2762

Trinidad and Tobago

2 Newbold Street
St. Clair, Port-of-Spain
Trinidad, W.I.
Tel: (809) 622-4995-7, 622-3849
Fax: (809) 628-9180

Puerto Rico

Plaxa Scotiabank, Suite 907
273, Ponce de Leon Avenue
Hato Rey
Puerto Rico 00918
Tel: (809) 758-3933, 758-2645, 758-2744
Fax: (809) 758-4011

United States

866 Second Avenue
New York, New York 10017
USA
Tel: (212) 371-4800
Telex: 661948 JAMPRO
Fax: (212) 751-5819

1020 Ingraham Building
25 South East 2nd Avenue
Miami, Florida 33131
USA
Tel: (305) 371-4405
Fax: (305) 371-8599

1155 15th Street, N.W., Suite 811
Washington, D.C. 20005
USA
Tel: (202) 452-9283, 452-9284
Fax: (202 452-9285

Canada

214 King Street West, Suite 214
Toronto, Ontario M5H 3S6
Canada
Tel: (416) 593-6233
Telex: 06219738
Fax: (416) 593-4821

Europe

50 St. James' Street
London SWIA 1JT
England
Tel: (01) 629-5477
Telex: 262820 JAMCO G

avenue Louise 375
1050 Brussels
Belgium
Tel: (322) 641-7923, 641-7924
Telex: 24300 BCFLTD
Fax: (322) 648-6413

Hong Kong

Suite 1119, Jardine House
1 Connaught Place, Central
Hong Kong
Tel: (5) 263243
Telex: 86624 JNIP
Fax: (5) 810-4381

Jamaica's Location

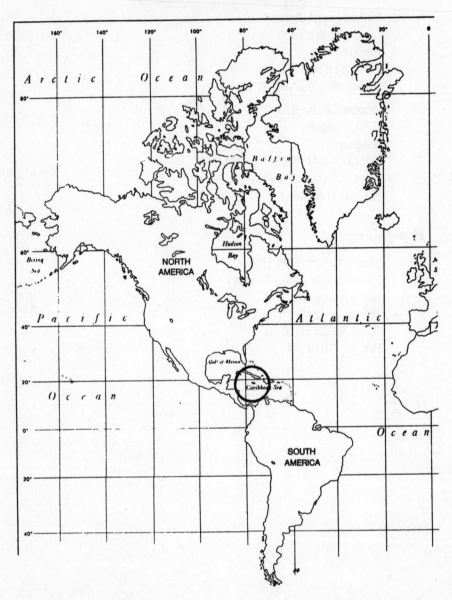

Chapter Ten
Japan: The Best-Kept Secret

This chapter contains broad information about Japan which the reader will find useful.

Japan's total land area is small, less than $\frac{1}{20}$ the size of the United States, or about the same size as California. Japan is a group of more than 3,900 islands stretching in a long chain along the eastern coats of Asia, near China, Korea, and the Soviet Union. The entire island chain, from Okinawa to Hokkaido, is about 2,000 miles long.

Most Japanese live on four main islands: Honshu, Shikoku, Kyushu, and Hokkaido.

The climate ranges from subarctic to subtropic. In the north the summers are cool and the winters harsh and snowy, while in the south the summers are hot and winters mild.

With over 121 million people, Japan is the world's seventh most populous nation. Because of its small land area, Japan is also one of the world's most densely populated countries, possess 325 persons per square kilometer, compared with 25 in the United States.

Unlike many other nations, Japan has a relatively homogeneous society. All Japanese have similar racial characteristics, speak the same language, and share essentially the same cultural tradition. Japan's cities are extremely crowded. Tokyo, the nation's capital and the largest city, has a population of 11.9 million, and over 30 million, if suburban prefectures are included. Tokyo is so big that it has no single "downtown" area, but a series of major urban centers.

Tokyo is extremely expensive. For example, an average square foot cost for space in commercial districts is $1250. Japan ranks second in the free world in economic production (GNP), behind only the U.S. It is a leading world producer of automobiles, consumer electronics, steel, cameras, watches, computers, industrial machinery, chemicals, rubber, plastics, and other important products.

Overall, Japan's economy compares favorably with that of the U.S. in terms of technology and sophistication. Most workers in Japan (57%) are employed in service industries, such as wholesale and retail trade, banking, insurance, and transportation. About a third (34%) work in manufacturing industries, while only 9% work in primary industries such as farming, fishing, and forestry.

Japan has very few natural resources and must import large quantities of raw materials, including iron ore, copper, bauxite, cotton and wool, food grains, and petroleum. To pay for these essential imports, Japan must export manufactured goods overseas. Japan is one of the world's largest trading nations, accounting for about 10% of all trade (import and export) in the world. For this reason, Japan is very dependent upon a peaceful and stable world trading system.

Japan exports its products to virtually all nations. About 35% of all Japanese exports go to the USA, which is Japan's most important trading partner. Japan, for the U.S., is second only to Canada in terms of trading partners. U.S.–Japanese trade exceeds $120 billion annually.

Japan leads the world in production and use of robots. But Japanese workers are highly trained and dedicated to their work and very loyal to their companies. Companies regard their employees as "members of the family," and usually hire them with the expectation that they will remain with the company for their entire career. Workers are very rarely laid-off or fired.

The manufacturing wage is now comparable to that of the U.S. and is substantially higher than in France or Italy. Japanese workers are typically organized into company unions, rather than industry-wide unions. For example, there us a Toyota union, Honda union, etc.

Japan became a modern industrial nation in about a century, faster than any other country in history. It is ironic to note that Japan has emerged from a state of borrowed and adapted technology from the U.S. and other advanced countries to a leader providing technological assistance to American and European firms.

Currency: The monetary currency is the Japanese Yen. As of February, 1990 the exchange rate of Yen was 145.60 Yen equal to one U.S. Dollar.

Japan has a multi-party political system, featuring six major parties. Japan's Liberal Democratic Party has been consistently in power since the 1950s.

And the bottom line is, as noted earlier in this chapter, Japan is gaining an economic and industrial strength unparalleled by any other nation in the world. Japan arose from the ashes of defeat in World War II after the infamous A-bombs dropped on Hiroshima and Nagasaki. Before the war the Japanese were considered the sub-contractors of world economics and they offered their services to the developed western countries to produce and manufacture in Japan. Almost without warning Japan transformed itself into an industrial and economic tower of strength threatening America's dominance in high technology pioneering and production.

In light of this situation America enforced a "state of emergency" by imposing import quotas and raising duties. However, there are many loopholes and it is politically difficult to keep out products such as automobiles and electronic goods which are either made better in Japan or not made at all in the U.S.

The U.S. Government is now looking over carefully all U.S. investment proposals in Japan. The Japanese government, on the other hand, has been encouraging their businesses to invest in foreign lands. As a result, the Japanese have recently gone on a "shopping spree" purchasing major real estate parcels, such as Rockefeller Center in New York City. The Japanese have also publicly lectured the U.S. on its failures in education, science, technology, and social life. Reaction from Americans has been vociferous, and the Japanese government is now looking over its policy to see if, perhaps, they have "overdone it a bit."

Japan's standard of living is rising as fast as its economy, and it is becoming expensive to manufacture there. It is cheaper to produce in other parts of South East Asia, or even in the United States, and to ship goods back to Japan. Western countries have made changes in their respective immigration laws to try and withstand the Japanese onslaught.

Obtaining information on citizenship in Japan was almost impossible for us because the feat is itself rare. After many attempts and inquiries with Japanese authorities it wasn't difficult to conclude that Japan is not at all interested in immigration and there is no official publication on the subject.

What is evident is that in Japan investment will not produce a passport. The Japanese are interested in "brains"—talented people from various fields like the sciences, medicine, and education. There have been foreigners who have lived in Japan and contributed to the advancement of Japanese science and life. To show appreciation for their contributions to Japan these "brains" are granted citizenship out of honor and respect.

Additional and Useful Information About Japan

How to Say and Write It in Japanese

English	Japanese	kanji[a]	hiragana[b]
human being	ningen	人間	にんげん
man	otoko	男	おとこ
woman	onna	女	おんな
child	kodomo	子供	こども
friend	tomodachi	友達	ともだち
teacher	sensei	先生	せんせい
dog	inu	犬	いぬ
cat	neko	猫	ねこ
book	hon	本	ほん
one	ichi	一	いち
two	ni	二	に

three	san	三	さん
four	shi	四	し
five	go	五	ご
six	roku	六	ろく
seven	shichi	七	しち
eight	hachi	八	はち
nine	kyu	九	きゅう
ten	ju	十	じゅう
good morning	ohayo	お早う	おはよう
hello	konnichi wa	今日は	こんにちは
good evening	konban wa	今晩は	こんばんは
good night	oyasumi nasai	お休みなさい	おやすみなさい
good-bye	sayonara	左様なら	さようなら
thank you	arigato	有難う	ありがとう
welcome	irasshyai	いらっしゃい	いらっしゃい
excuse me	gomen nasai	御免なさい	ごめんなさい

[a]Chinese characters used in Japanese
[b]Japanese *hiragana* script

Addresses

Central government and its affiliated organizations

Ministry of International Trade and Industry (MITI)
Office for the Promotion of the Foreign Investment in Japan
1-3-1 Kasumigaseki,
Chiyoda-ku,
Tokyo 100, Japan
Tel: 03-501-6623

Ministry of International Trade and Industry (MITI)
Industrial Location Guidance Div.
1-3-1 Kasumigaseki,
Choyoda-ku,
Tokyo 100, Japan
Tel: 03-501-0645

Japan External Trade Organization (JETRO)
Investment Promotion Div.
2-2-5 Toranomon,
Mitato-ku
Tokyo 105, Japan
Tel: 03-582-5571

Japan Regional Development Corporation (JRDC)
Sales Promotion Div
3-8-1 Kasumigaseki,
Chiyoda-ku,
Tokyo 100, Japan
Tel: 03-501-5211

Center for Inducement of Industry to Rural Areas
Operations Div.
1-11-38 Nagatacho,
Chiyoda-ku,
Tokyo, Japan
Tel: 03-502-2361

Japan Industrial Location Center
Operation Div.
1-4-2 Toranomon,
Minato-ku
Tokyo 105, Japan
Tel: 03-502-2361

The Japan Development Bank
International Dept.
1-9-1 Otemachi,
Chiyoda-ku
Tokyo 100, Japan
Tel: 03-270-3211

The Hokkaido-Tohoku Development Corporation
Project Development Div.
1-9-3 Otemachi,
Chiyoda-ku
Tokyo 100, Japan
Tel: 03-270-1651

Japan Technomart Foundation
8 Fl. Mori Bldg No. 33, 3-8-21
Toranomon,
Minato-ku
Tokyo, Japan
Tel: 03-432-6061

Japan External Trade organization (JETRO)
2-5 Toranomon 2-chome,
Minato-ku,
Tokyo 5, Japan
Tel: 03-582-5511

Japan Overseas Enterprise Association
Hanshin Green Bldg. 6-20,
Kyobashi 2-chome,
Chuo-ku,
Tokyo 104, Japan
Tel: 03-567-9271

Japan Patent Information center
Bansui Bldg. 5-16,
Toranomon 1-chome,
Minato-ku,
Tokyo 105, Japan
Tel: 03-503-6181

Japan Institute of Invention and Innovation
9-14 Toranomon 2-chome,
Monato-ku,
Tokyo 105, Japan
Tel: 03-502-0511

Japan Foreign Trade Council, Inc.
World Trade Center Bldg. 1-4,
Hamamatsucho 2-chome,
Minato-ku
Tokyo 105, Japan
Tel: 03-287-1221

Japan Regional Development Corporation
Toranomon Mitsui Bldg. 8-1,
Kasumigaseki 3-chome
Chiyoda-ku,
Tokyo 100, Japan
Tel: 03-501-5211

Federation of Economic Organizations (KEIDANREN)
9-3 Otemachi 1-chome,
Chiyoda-ku,
Tokyo 100, Japan
Tel: 03-279-1411

Japan's Location

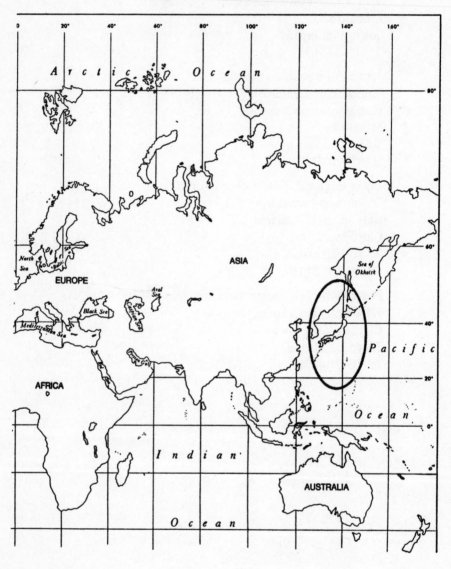

Chapter Eleven
New Zealand: Automatic Double Passport Benefits

Introduction—The Land and People

New Zealand has a land area of 27 million hectares making it similar in size to Japan or Great Britain. the population of 3.3 million is English speaking. There is a significant Polynesian population: this consists of Maori people, the first settlers of New Zealand, and Pacific Islanders, many of whom have come to New Zealand in the last few decades.

The city of Auckland is the main center of commerce and industry. Wellington is the capital city and the center of government. Other cities and regions offer a variety of attractive business and social opportunities.

The climate is temperate, without extremes of heat or cold. Most areas experience more than 2000 hours of sunshine a year along with ample rainfall.

New Zealand is situated in the Pacific Basin 1600 km to the east of Australia. It has close political, economic, and cultural relations with Australia and the Pacific Island neighbors.

Government

The government of New Zealand is modeled on the British parliamentary system, with elections based upon universal adult suffrage. There is a party approach to politics and an independent judiciary. New Zealand is a constitutional monarchy, the Head of State—Her Majesty, Queen Elizabeth II—is represented within the country by a resident Governor-General.

Economic and Social Indicators

The New Zealand Dollar, or "Kiwi," is a floating currency. As of February, 1990 its value was: one NZ$ equal to 0.559 U.S. Dollar.

Together, Australia and New Zealand form an affluent and sophisticated market of more than 19 million people. New Zealand is close to the huge and rapidly developing markets of East and South East Asia.

New Zealand had a gross domestic product in excess of NZ 53 billion in 1986–87.

New Zealand's prosperity is dependent on external trade. For the five years ended March 31, 1988 exports of goods and services averaged 35% of G.D.P. In the same period imports of goods and services averaged 34% of G.D.P.

Increased export returns and reduced imports have meant that for the year ended November 1988 New Zealand's merchandise trade balance was approximately NZ 2 billion. The current deficit for the year ended September 1988 fell to approximately NZ$797 million.

Industry

1. New Zealand is one of the largest exporters of meat, wool and dairy products in the world. There are 70 million sheep and 8 million cattle earning more than 50 percent of the country's export income.

2. After agriculture, forestry is New Zealand's most important industry. It is based mainly on 657,000 hectares of exotic forest—mainly quick-growing pine.

3. Gold and coal were the historically important minerals. Gold production is down to 10,000 ounces a year. There are large deposits of coal with current production at 2.2 million tons. Large deposits of titano-magnetite iron sands on the North Island west coast supply local industry while concentrate are shipped to Japan. Natural gas, also on the North Island west coast, supplies major North island cities.

4. Manufacturing industries have grown rapidly in importance and their net output constitutes 26% of real gross domestic product. Some 25% of the total labor force is employed directly in manufacturing, and while there is a trend to larger manufacturing units, the average staff numbers are only 31 persons.

Traditionally, Britain has been New Zealand's major trading partner. In recent years this trading dependence has been eased and trade expanded with Australia, the USA, Japan and other countries.

Professional fees

Accountants: A survey of public accountancy practices of fees at March 31, 1988 produced the following national averages (excluding GST):

Qualified accountant: $51 per hour
General partner: $78 per hour
Specialist accountant: $88 per hour

Lawyers: In Wellington an experienced lawyer, specializing in corporate law charges approximately $220 per hour. To establish a company in New Zealand and obtain OIC consent generally costs $1000 to $1500. In a provincial center, Hamilton, the services of a lawyer dealing in company law would average $160 an hour, excluding GST.

Immigration, Business and Investment Opportunities

Business immigrants are welcome in New Zealand as a source of new commercial ideas and entrepreneurial skills. You can consider New Zealand on the list of countries that provide citizenship and subsequently a passport in return for an investment. Under the Business Immigration Policy (B.I.P.) permanent residency status is granted to people who are willing to invest at least $125,000 (approximately NZ$200,000) for their personal and business establishment. However, applications for investment are scrutinized for intent, authenticity, legitimacy, and viability. A direct intervention is needed by the investor in the setting up of the venture, management, etc. Upon presenting your application you must show your personal financial records and character references, as well as an outline of the proposed business activity. You will also have to demonstrate how your project will impact the local community in various aspects, including employment opportunities, diversify trade, and enhance New Zealand's exports.

Three years after obtaining permanent residency you are entitled to citizenship and a passport. And, most importantly, a New Zealand citizen immediately "inherits" most of Australian rights.

Normally, investment in New Zealand is less costly than in Australia and the benefits far greater. There is a great link between New Zealand and Australia which goes beyond mere membership in the British Commonwealth. The two countries share language, cultural similarities, economic structuring and mutual assistance. New Zealand is sometimes referred as a suburb of Australia. It's a pity, perhaps, as New Zealand has its own strong national identity.

For further information regarding immigration, business and investment opportunities you could apply to any New Zealand embassy, consulate, or high commission.

Useful Addresses and Information

Addresses

Overseas Investment Commission
P.O. Box 2498
Wellington, New Zealand
Tel: (04) 772-029
Telex: RESBANK NZ3368
Fax: (04) 738-554

Business Development Service
Ministry of Commerce

Auckland
P.O. Box 4259
Tel: 909) 33-189
Fax: (09) 33-349

Wellington
P.O. Box 1473
Tel: (04) 720-030
Telex: TRADIND NZ31-530
Fax: (04) 734-638

New Zealand Chambers of Commerce
P.O. Box 11-043
Wellington
Tel: (04) 723-376
Telex: NZ 3714 CHACO
Fax: (04) 711-767

Immigration Division
Department of Labour
Box 4130
Wellington
Tel: (04) 739-100
Telex: NZ3441 SECLAB
Fax: (04) 712-118

New Zealand Trade Development Board
Head Office
P.O. Box 10-341
Wellington
Tel: (04) 742-600
Telex/Datex: NZ31835
Fax: (04) 733-193

Useful Publications

Doing Business in New Zealand
Ernst & Whinney
Fax: (04) 722-162

Doing Business in New Zealand
(Available in Japanese translation)
Price Waterhouse
Fax (04) 720-207

Investment & Business in New Zealand
Peat Marwick Mitchell
Fax: (04) 723-181

Investment in New Zealand—Policies and Opportunities
Bank of New Zealand
Fax: (04) 729-076

General Guide to Overseas Investment in New Zealand
Bell Gully Buddle Weir
Fax: (04) 733-845

A Guide to Doing Business in New Zealand
Kensington Swan
Fax: (09) 394-276

Buying Property and Commencing Business in New Zealand
Russell McVeagh McKenzi Bartlett & Co
Fax: (04) 732-730

Legal Aspects of Doing Business in New Zealand
Rudd Watts & Stone
Fax: (09) 31-169

Business Migration to New Zealand
Coopers & Lybrand
Fax: (09) 278-7669

New Zealand; A Guide for New Settlers
($NZ18.14 plus postage overseas)
New Zealand Diplomatic Posts or
Government Printing Office
Fax: (04) 734-943

1988 New Zealand/Japan Trade Yearbook
(In Japanese/English)
New Zealand Embassy, Tokyo

1988 New Zealand/Korea Trade Yearbook
(In Korean/English)
New Zealand Embassy, Seoul

Embassies, Consulates, and High Commissions

Australia, Austria, Bahrain, Belgium, Canada, Chile, China, Cook Islands, Fiji, France, Germany, Greece, Hong Kong, India, Indonesia, Iran, Iraq, Italy, Japan, Korea, Malaysia, Mexico, Netherlands, New Caledonia, Niue, Papua, New Guinea, Peru, Philippines, Saudi Arabia, Singapore, Solomon Islands, Switzerland, Thailand, Tonga, USSR, United Kingdom, USA Western Samoa, and Zimbabwe.

New Zealand's Location

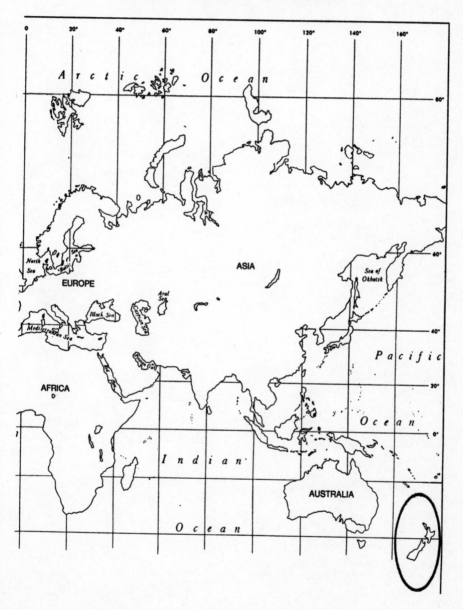

Chapter Twelve
Philippines: Land of "Limited Opportunities"

General Information About the Country and People

The Philippines Archipelago lies off the southern coast of the Asian mainland surrounded by the Pacific Ocean on the east, the South China Sea on the west and north, and the Celebes Sea on the south.

Topography

The archipelago consists of about 7,100 islands, 11 of which are major land masses, spread over an area of 300,439 square kilometers. The topography is highly diverse with major mountain ranges and large plains and plateaus. The country has an extensive coastline with numerous bays and harbors and navigable inland river systems.

There are only two seasons: the dry season from about November to April and the wet season from May to October.

History

The first inhabitants of the Philippines were Negritos, Indonesians, and the Malay from the neighboring islands with the Chinese coming in as traders and settlers. From 1521, the year in which Ferdinand Magellan laid claim on the Philippines for Spain, until 1946 the country was under foreign rule; the Spaniards from 1521 to 1898; the Americans from 1898 to 1942; the Japanese from 1942 to 1944; and again the Americans from 1944 to 1946. The Philippines gained its independence from the United States on July 4, 1946.

Government

The Philippines has operated under a republican form of government since its independence, except for a period of martial rule from 1972 to 1981. The present head of state, Corazon Aquino, was ushered into office by a peaceful revolution against the former president in February, 1986. A new constitution was ratified in February, 1987. Elections for the bicameral legislature were held in May, 1987 and for the local government positions in January, 1988.

The people

Filipinos, according to the most recent official census, number 57.4 million. Population growth is estimated at 2.7% annually, and the number of Filipinos is expected to top 75.2 million by the year 2000. Metro Manila will continue to be the most densely populated area in the country, holding over 14 of every 1200 Filipinos in the Philippines.

Filipinos are basically of the Malay race mixed with Chinese and Spanish ancestries. There are 11 cultural and racial groups, each with its own language in business, government, schools and everyday communication. Filipino, based primarily on the Tagalog language, is the national language. There are 11 languages and 87 dialects in the archipelago.

Aside from English, Spanish is another foreign language spoken fluently by a number of Filipinos, along with Arabic, Chinese, and Nippongo.

The labor force is estimated at around 23.52 million, 91.6% of which is employed. Of those employed, 43.76% are agricultural, animal husbandry, fishery, and forestry workers. Around 22.42% are production workers, transport equipment operators and laborers; 13.73% are in sales, 9.32% are service workers, and 6.71% are in professional and managerial jobs. The remaining 4% hold clerical jobs.

Currency: The Philippines' monetary unit is the Peso. As of February, 1990 the foreign exchange rate was 22.17 Philipine Pesos equal to one U.S. Dollar.

The Philippine authorities might welcome those who are willing to invest at least $75,000 in various fields which the government considers essential to its economic development but the benefits to the investor are minimal. The government does not give any special consideration to the investor, in reality. However, a person can receive an "investor's resident" status, which does not differ much from a student or a foreign worker's residence permit. The road to citizenship is long, usually 10 years, and the entrepreneur has no advantage over a teacher at a public school or one who weds a Philippine citizen.

A better chance is for one who would create jobs for local citizenry or help in developing the economy. Another better and easier route is for real estate development, no matter what the scale of business. The general impression is that although the Philippines welcomes foreign investors, it doesn't regard the individual investor very highly. For those who are really interested in this part of the world, a passport is obtainable even after five years.

Here are names and addresses which can be quite useful:

Overseas Representatives

Office of the Investment Attaché
Tokyo: 11-24 Nampeidai-machi
Shibuya-Ku

Office of the Investment Attaché
Bonn: Argelandstrasse 1
5300 Bonn 1

Office of the Philippine Trade Commissioners
San Francisco: 447 Surer, Suite 516

London: IA Cumberland House
Kensington Court

Council for Investments
385 Sen. Gil J. Puyat Avenue
Makati, Metro Manila
PHILIPPINES
Tel. Nos. 86-84-03/86-78-95
Telex 45555 BOI PM/122661 BOI PH
Fax 632-851166

Philippines' Location

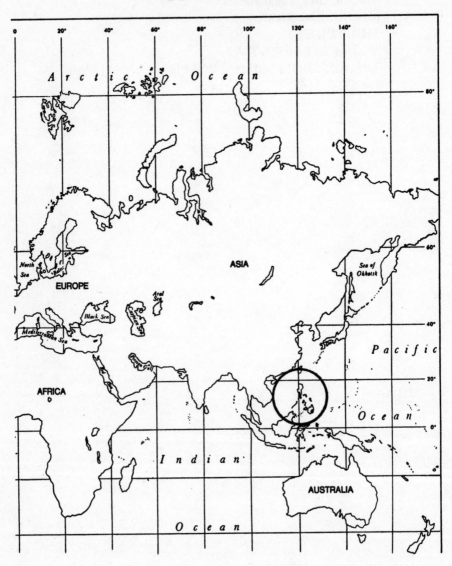

Chapter Thirteen
Portugal: Vacation Your Way to E.E.C. Passport Benefits

Introduction

Portugal is a country with an area of 92.1 thousand square kilometers with a population of approximately ten million inhabitants.

It is located in the southwestern tip of Europe at the junction of major routes, between America and Africa.

Portugal has:

- Easy means of communications, since mainly English, French, and Spanish are commonly spoken
- Social and political stability in a system of parliamentary democracy where, since July 1987, a single party—the Social Democrats, has the absolute majority

- A system of guarantees and incentives where foreign capital companies are granted equal conditions to any Portuguese one

Portugal is now experiencing a period of relaxed growth. Unemployment is now about 5.1%, down 8.5% from 1984, and inflation was reduced to 9.5% in 1988 from 25% in 1983 and 1984.

Currency: The Portugal monetary unit is the Escudo. As of February, 1990 the exchange rate was 146 Portuguese Escudos to one U.S. Dollar.

Portugal is discovering new potentials derived from its integration in Europe, as Europe is discovering that the south has an important role in its unity. Nine hundred years of Portuguese history, are, perhaps, the best proof that this nation will be able to rediscover itself now within the bounds of its primitive frontiers.

Portugal is considered one of the top countries by business people and entrepreneurs in which to hold a second and foreign passport. Although there is a five-year residency period, citizenship is achieved relatively easily. There are many attractive inexpensive investment opportunities in Portugal which provide short-term payback with high profits.

Many entrepreneurs jumped on the bandwagon after realizing that foreigners can acquire real estate property very easily (in fact, it is the easiest country in which to obtain a passport from within the member countries of the European Economic Community) and which is not the case in most other countries. Portugal is guided by the old Roman law which equates the land owner with being a "man of means." This official attitude enables the new "land owner" to achieve citizenship in five years.

It is indeed highly interesting to note that the acquisition of real estate property as a route towards gaining citizenship in Portugal is not parallel to the "regular" process. "New" land owners enjoy special rights and privileges, including citizenship, granted under 2000 year old regulations which have stood the test of time and the courts.

The Portuguese authorities might eventually alter the regulations regarding foreign investments in real estate because of external pressure from a number of sources, mainly within Europe. But as long as these procedures take time individuals who are keen on acquiring a Portuguese passport are still entering through the "front door."

Portugal (a member of the European Common Market, or E.E.C.) does not require continuous permanent residency during the waiting period and once citizenship and a passport are obtained, the holder is free to work and live anywhere in any E.E.C. country.

A Portuguese passport holder could, without difficulty, become a permanent or temporary citizen of the former Portuguese colony—Brazil. Most other countries in the world recognize the Portuguese passport and don't require visas for entry.

Options available to the foreign investor in Portugal usually fall into two areas: recreational property in tourist spots or buying property anywhere in the country with at least a dwelling on it. The minimum required for investment is $35,000. This is cheaper than a recreational property in most of the Western countries. In Portugal payments can even be spread over a few years.

There are a number of recreational resorts in Portugal seeking foreign investors. The sales pitch includes the point that investment in the property can lead to a passport in a couple of years. After signing the contract for the recreational dwelling unit one must apply at the nearest Portuguese Embassy and apply for residency. Among the documents needed are proof of annual income of at least $15,000 or $1250 monthly. It is not required to transfer this income to Portugal. If one can not come up with such papers the buyer must prove possession of real estate and other property of equal value elsewhere.

The next step is to travel to Lisbon, the capital of Portugal, to receive residency papers which will be ready within a few weeks from the time of application. Residency permits must be renewed annually in person or by means of a representative. The investor may include his or her spouse, sons and daughters under 18 years (only if they are still single). If the investor chooses to reside in Portugal after gaining citizenship, additional relatives, not of the immediate family, could be included for permanent residency leading to citizenship.

There is a cloud in this silver lining of Portugal's otherwise attractive citizenship and passport route: Sufficient Portuguese must be spoken to pass a verbal test which can be taken at any Portuguese embassy around the world. A Berlitz course or other means of study can provide enough fluency to pass the test. Word has it, however, that the test is always the same one, year after year, so that if you fail it the first time, just remember the questions for the next time.

After gaining the passport it is possible to sell the property. A wise investment could cover all the expenses and result in a very decent profit!

There is another type of Portuguese document available which allows a foreigner to travel under the rights and privileges of the Portuguese government. This is called a Portuguese alien passport, to which a visa must be attached. On this travel document an entire family may be listed and the Portuguese don't insist upon relinquishment of the other passport in your possession. There is a firm that deals in foreign acquisitions, investments and development, mainly in Portugal, but in many other places around the world:

Montpelier, Ltd.
15/F Ruttonjee House
11 Duddell St
Central, Hong-Kong
Tel: 5-231823, 5-264858
Telex: 74783 MIB HX

The firm has a partnership office in London:

The Tiller Group
33 Berkeley House
Hay Hill
London W1X 7LG
Tel: (01) 4999900, (01) 6292872

The firm provides extensive aid and can even obtain legal assistance in Lisbon for the acquisition of real estate. The company provides glossy and provocative brochures concerning investing in real estate, and a booklet about obtaining a passport. They also add a warning that Portuguese officials might eventually change their rules and regulations. At the moment there are three projects with purchasing options on offer (they might even be sold out already) from the firm in sun-drenched Portuguese resorts:

Project # 1: The Waterside Village of Luz, a new project near Lagos. Each apartment overlooks the ocean and there is a selection of 1, 2, or 3 bedroom apartments at a starting price of $55,000. Included in the price is the privilege of membership in a nearby exclusive country club. The address for correspondence:

> Travessa Do Forno 4
> 8600 Lagos
> Portugal
> Tel: 082-63721
> Telex: 57675 ALPART

Project # 2: Vale de Centianes. Situated near a town by the sea called Carvoiero, where a new group of apartment hotels has been constructed. 1 or 2 bedroom apartments start at $52,000. For direct correspondence:

> Algarvesol—Saral
> Apartado 107
> 8520 Portimão, Portugal

Project # 3: Balaia Village, near Albufeira, overlooking the sea.

This attractive area is situated back to back with the luxurious Balaia Hotel, a 5 Star-rated hotel. The 1, 2, or 3 bedroom apartments start at $65,000 and there is an option of a lease back.

Addresses for further information:

> Balaia Village
> Albufeira
> Algarve, Portugal
> Tel: 55236
> Telex: 56254 Camper P

or

Av. Duque de Loule
47–32 Esq
1000 Lisbon, Portugal
Tel: 572142, 556046, 540138

It is indeed quite a strange thing that Portuguese embassies and commercial consulates around the world never seem to reveal much information about investment opportunities in Portugal. We suggest that you accumulate more detailed data through:

Ministry of Foreign Affairs
Lisboa (Lisbon), Portugal

Portugal's Location

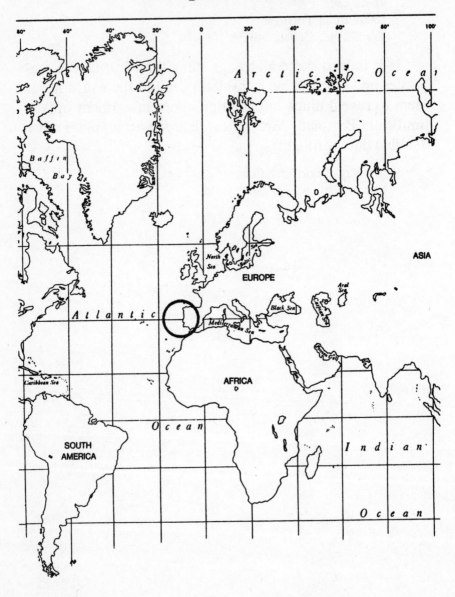

Chapter Fourteen
South Africa: Foreign Investments and Benefits

General Information About the Country and People

The total area of South Africa is 113.9 million hectares. The country lies almost entirely in the temperate zone with a average number of hours of sunshine per day varying from 7.5 to 9.5.

South Africa is a sovereign independent republic comprising four provinces: Cape of Good Hope, Transvaal, Orange Free State, and Natal. The Republic was established on May 31, 1961.

The People and Their Lifestyle

The South African way of life has been largely shaped by the mild and healthy climate. South Africans are open minded, sturdy and independent, fond of outdoor living and sport, hospitable and free and easy in social relationships. Of course, we are talking about White South Africa which has ruled the country since the Afrikaners from Europe settled the territory. White South Africans are descended mainly from four European nations; the British, French, Dutch, and Germans, who have all left their mark of there national customs on the South African way of life.

South Africa is located on the southern tip of the African continent and is one of the wealthiest nations in the world in terms of natural resources. The bulk of the country's income is derived from these resources:

Apart from gold, of which 77% of the world production is mined in South Africa, diamonds, coal, copper, iron, platinum, vanadium, chrome, manganese, asbestos, vermiculite, uranium, antinomy, and numerous other minerals are mined extensively.

Modern farming methods make South Africa self sufficient in food production. The following are some of the agricultural products produced extensively: maize, wheat, sugar, tobacco, fruit, vegetables, flowers, wine, cattle, sheep, and wool, karakul pelts, mohair, and timber. Much of these products are exported.

In South Africa there exists the ideal climate for agricultural growth and in this regard, the country is quite developed.

South Africa is regarded today as a self-made country in that the supply of their own demands is met by domestically stimulated means; industrial and agricultural. The country does not have to depend on foreign aid and relies on the strength of its own markets. This self-reliance is born out of basic necessity.

The country's totalitarian system of apartheid with white racist power dominating the lives of the millions more black inhabitants has invited economic sanctions and isolation from many countries in the world. Shunned for it extreme racism, South Africa treasures its enormous reserves of gold, diamonds, precious metals, and other commodities which the rest of the world needs and wants. Because of this wealth in natural resources, South Africa can, quite easily, take care of itself.

In the last several years both internal and external pressures on the white minority government have led to small, but significant changes towards the breakdown of the oppressive system of apartheid. These changes, mostly in the lifting of some restrictions of movement by the non-white population, give little, except hope, that perhaps one day, without violent revolution, equality will be achieved.

Without pressure on the government of South Africa there would be little motivation to give up what the Afrikaner farmers who settled in the country fought so hard to achieve. The country's great economic wealth and independence, military strength, achievements in educational, medical, and scientific spheres are the undeniable result of the dedication and tenacity of the Afrikaner character. Unfortunately, these achievements were all made at the expense and exploitation of the black population.

As the pressures and demands for change take place the government of South Africa is slowly allowing blacks to become involved in almost every sector of society. Realizing that the future of the country depends on its return to the world community, the government has become suddenly desperate for foreign investment.

As an indication of this need the government declared

a lucrative offer for foreign investors called "the Financial Rand."

This offer sets up two rates to the national currency; the Commercial Rand and the Financial Rand.

Currency: The monetary unit of South Africa is the Rand. As of February, 1990 the foreign exchange rate was 2.53 Rands equal to one U.S. Dollar.

What Is the Financial Rand?

The South African Financial Rand is a non-resident investment currency and can be seen as a pool of restricted Rands belonging to non-residents and new immigrants who arrived in south Africa on or after February 9, 1985.

The financial Rand was reintroduced by the government in 1985 to discourage the outflow of non-resident investment from South Africa while at the same time encouraging new non-resident investment in south Africa.

Commercial Rand

The Commercial Rands are subject to exchange control limitations and are used by South African residents to buy dollars from the Reserve Bank.

The commercialized Rand, on the other hand, reflects the country's existing economic position, state of our current and capital accounts and the ability of South Africa to generate sufficient net exports to meet its immediate requirements.

Financial Rand

Financial Rands are exchanged for dollars only outside of South Africa through the external mechanism of the so-called financial Rand pool.

The financial Rand therefore reflects the confidence or lack thereof that foreign investors have in South Africa. The level of confidence may be measured by the extent of the discount to the commercial Rand.

No currency or other assets actually leave South Africa, but the ownership of financial Rand balances passes between one non-resident and another. These deals do not impact on the Reserve Bank's foreign exchange reserves, but are financed entirely by financial Rand bookkeeping.

Uses of the financial Rand

- Investment in South African securities by non-residents. The securities may be exported only after they have been restrictively endorsed "non-resident"
- Subscription to additional issues of quoted shares by non-residents
- Bank charges charged to non-resident bank accounts
- Taking up shares in new non-quoted companies by non-residents
- Purchase of property by non-residents
- Immigrants—settling in allowances

To make things clearer, a foreign investor, or any new immigrant may invest in South Africa any "hard" foreign currency, in a financial redevelopment program called the Financial Rand. There is a 50–100% difference in rates to the Commercial Rand. In short, the investment in South Africa would be 30–50% lower because of the better rate.

The other side to this "coin" is when you wish to liquidate your investment you will receive the lower rate. However, this occurs only in case you are officially required to extract your investment from South Africa.

Immigration and Receiving the South African Passport

The minimal sum required for immigration to South Africa ranges between $50,000–$100,000. This is very flexible, however.

From the permanent resident status, which takes a couple of months, to the request of citizenship and passport, a five year residency is required in the country.

After the immigration application is approved, new immigrants immediately receive Financial Rand benefits. The initial sums are fixed—

Individual: R100,000
Family: R200,000

Larger sums can certainly be deposited. From knowledgeable people we found that there are some circumstances which enable the applicant to obtain authorization for a larger transaction, up to R1,000,000.

A question arises about the desirability of the South African passport. Is it worth it? It is, after all, one of the least respected documents in the world community. The answer must be regarded as strictly personal and up to each investor.

In any case, many entrepreneurs do their business there, which is attributed to the benefits given by the government, especially the Financial Rand Program.

For further official information about South Africa contact the embassy nearest you. In particular, if you are interested in the opportunities of investing contact the investments consultant of the South African Government who is well informed about the Financial Rand Program.

South Africa's Location

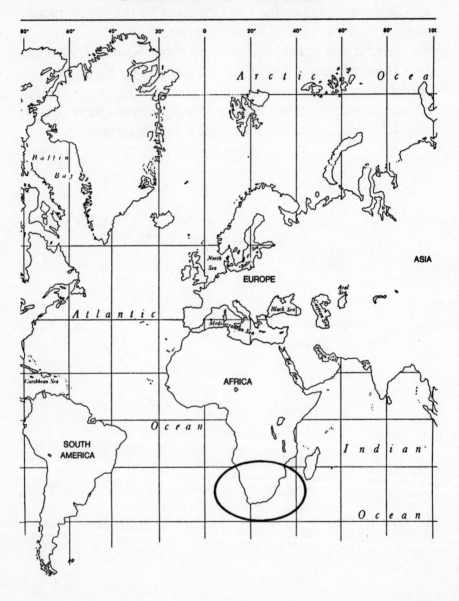

PART II

PART II

Chapter Fifteen
Finding Investments Abroad

Finding suitable and profitable investments abroad can be complicated without good connections and contacts. But, more importantly, reliable and timely information is the best bet in insuring financial success and ultimately in obtaining citizenship in another country for the purposes of obtaining a foreign passport.

Probably the best and surest way to get this information is through the diplomatic representatives. Usually there is an economic attaché in every embassy who will gladly be of assistance and service. Every embassy has a library with addresses of companies, government offices and other institutions, private or public.

After you have the basic idea of what you need you can proceed to call upon the specific diplomatic representative at the embassy or consulate nearest you. Their job is to assist and guide investors and usually these representatives do their jobs flawlessly.

There is still no substitute for a lengthy stay in the country itself in order to look things over first hand. In the various economic or general newspapers one can usually find helpful information on investment opportunities.

Another excellent source of reliable economic information is the international firm of Dun and Bradstreet which specializes in information about economic institutions of all sorts, public and private. They release information no matter if it's privileged or not. Information about an American or European body could be obtained on the same day. From other places it can take longer. Services are not inexpensive—an average subscription to the service is approximately $1000. Every request for data, or "information unit" as "D and B" puts it, is priced differently and is subtracted from the initial membership sum. The telephone number and address and all Dun and Bradstreet offices are readily available in the telephone directories in major cities around the world.

Other sources for more information on where to find good and reliable investment opportunities are two foreign journals. They produce information which is really quite amazing. The first publication is "The Economist Intelligence Unit"—EIU, a four times per year dossier on business projects in a given "unit." This journal as divided the world into 92 units and for each unit a full scale micro and macro report is issued four times yearly. For someone who is interested in a certain unit, previous issues are available to make a comprehensive analysis on that particular unit. The EIU gives a thorough understanding of the chances to succeed in a certain field or provides warnings of very high risk.

The subscription fee for one year (4 reports) currently is $110.00.

Subscription information:

The Economist Publications, Ltd.
40 Duke Street
London W1A 1DW

Another reliable British source of information is the monthly *South*. This journal specializes in third world economics and business investments. Economic supplements on various topics are regularly published. Inside are many business offers and propositions. In every issue and supplements are addresses for making contacts. Subscriptions are $48.00 annually.

Chapter Sixteen
How to Organize an Investment Plan

After selecting the country in which you wish to invest you will need to contact the embassy or economic representatives of that country in your own country, or in the new country itself. When you start negotiations with officials you should be as well prepared with authenticated documents as possible in writing with the following information:

1. Your business background, including precise details of your current activities or your firm's
2. Economic profile: a record of your finances, real estate holdings, etc. This is really a statement of your net worth
3. The proposed investment plan in detail and how it would be implemented
4. Timetable for your investment(s)

5. Your plans for immigration. This point is optional
    in certain cases, as some countries only require your
    money or a basic investment and don't inquire or
    "cross-examine" you on this point at all

Chapter Seventeen
Passport by Mail Order

It is possible. Not counterfeit passports, but official documents issued by certain countries to those investors who meet certain conditions. These countries are listed in the earlier chapter called "Investment Which Produces a Passport."

Some countries made an extra option of granting its passport to citizens who haven't set foot in the country. The passports are entirely legal, valid and usable.

This option is very vital to many investors who have no intention of emigration to another country. As you have read, most citizenships are achieved by a lengthy residency period in the desired country. But with this *passport by mail order* option an investor can avoid the whole residency ordeal. It still takes some time to actually receive the passport, but other valuable documents will issued to qualified investors in the interim.

Many charlatans have taken advantage of this and "issue" false passports which are worthless. These fake passports have limited effect because no immigration official in the world would be fooled by such a document. Its only value is for pretense and show.

Bolivia—A High Commission

The Bolivian option of obtaining a "postal passport" consists of two stages: an investment mainly in agriculture, and another larger investment in a private organization who would take care of the legal side of obtaining the passport.

The approximate range of investment needed starts at $25,000 and an additional $10,000 for any other family member. About 25% of the sum needed for investment can not be recovered and one must think of Bolivia as a means of gaining a passport and not a profitable business venture. The remaining amount of the investment goes to those who handle the paperwork. A passport could be issued in this manner between 18 months.

A quick calculation will show that the commissions in Bolivia are reasonable since they save the long trek there and the hiring of local legal sources. A company, based in London handles Bolivian passports by mail. The London firm only has a post office address:

Midi Limited
P.O.B. 261
NI IXJ London
Tel: 01/637 5277
Telex 299230 IFCENT

For more information, check ads in the International Herald Tribune or write to the diplomatic representative of Bolivia anywhere in the world.

Jamaica—After 5 Years

Jamaican authorities grant passports to investors 5 years after they have deposited their investment, even if they don't reside on the island. The Jamaican government through its Jamaican National Investment Program (JAMPRO) assist those who need a passport and are not able to travel to the island.

Conditions for investing in Jamaica have been detailed earlier in this guide. An initial amount of $120,000 is needed and the investor receives by mail a travel permit and a document of permanent residency in Jamaica. With these official Jamaican papers travelers from some countries who can not normally travel without obtaining entry visa to other countries can find ready access.

Actually, those who are content with the effectiveness of these official papers don't even have to apply for a passport; after 5 years the residency status would automatically be renewed.

The address for correspondence is the same as the JAMPRO mentioned in "Investment Which Produces a Passport."

Dominican Republic—Just Fly Away

Dominican Republic officials go out of their way towards investors who are willing to enhance the local economy. The investor must prove that absence from the Dominican Republic is essential to business matters. A passport by mail can be issued in 2–12 months, depending on the investor's relationship with the authorities.

This is a crucial point since whoever wishes to be a citizen normally must "do the residency period in the country." Authorities have been known to "look the other way" in order not to lose an investor.

Portugal—An Immediate Passport, If Needed

As we have seen, one can obtain a Portuguese passport without stepping foot in Portugal. All that is needed is the filing of an application at the nearest embassy. In countries where there is no Portuguese representation you can apply in another country or directly to the Foreign Office authorities in Lisbon. All that remains to be done is to wait for the mail to arrive! For a meager sum let someone else do the paperwork for you.

Let's say, for example, that the business transaction is the purchasing of an apartment unit. Any acquisition of a dwelling unit is suitable. After depositing at least ten percent of the total value the investor receives, in a bout two weeks, the contract for signature. After signing another 15–20% must be paid. The developer then co-signs. At this point the application for residency in Portugal can be made, based on the real estate contract. In addition to this application other documents must be submitted: a copy of the contract, proof of a monthly income of at least $1200, or the ownership of property (outside of Portugal) equivalent to a monthly income of the same amount. The investor's representative would then send all the papers to the "Foreigner's Department" at the Foreign Office in Lisbon. Those who purchase the real estate on the site could travel from the time-share property location to Lisbon and submit all the paperwork in person. In 6–9 months the temporary resident's visa is issued. In some cases the time can be substantially reduced. Within four months of receiving the temporary resident's visa the application for permanent status can be made at the Home Office in Lisbon. This period could be extended, depending on the individual case. The permanent residency paper is issued no later the 2–3 weeks after application. A question then arises, if the applicant must appear in person for the papers. Montpelier, Ltd., a company involved in the legalities informed us that it is reasonable to assume that an average law office could provide a legal excuse for the applicant not to appear in Portugal.

The price of assistance in gaining the permanent residency is around $750–1000. In the case where the investor does not want to travel to Portugal, the cost of representation can be substantially higher. But this sum would, in likelihood be less than cost of travel to and expenses in Portugal. An investor who wishes to add family members to residency documents may just submit the proper legal papers without the need for the entire family to travel to Portugal.

After getting the permanent residency documents, the investor could apply for a Portuguese alien passport. This document is usually given only to people with a restricted or limited passport or identification card. the investor must explain the particulars of his or her circumstances well. An

alien passport is just as valid as a regular passport, except that
a visa must be attached to it. And until the unrestricted passport is issued, after about five years, one must renew permanent residency every year. This could be handled by a lawyer
for about $250 each renewal. A quick accounting shows that
without the amount of the investment itself and travels to
Portugal, for as little as $2000 one can cut the Portuguese
bureaucracy to a minimum and obtain a passport.

Chapter Eighteen
The American Dream

To our surprise, the U.S. does not have any investors programs which may supply you with a passport. Due to various reasons the option of investing in American businesses has been eliminated, since 1976, as means shortening the time it takes to obtain a passport. This does not leave the investor any choice who must wait the 5-year period before applying for citizenship.

There are more restrictions in the U.S.: Half the period of residency prior to application for citizenship must actually be continuous in the U.S., and a minimum of 6 months each year.

And one cannot leave the U.S. for extensive periods without jeopardizing the residency period requirements. Also, the reputation of the American passport is becoming questionable and perhaps precarious to use in traveling to many parts of the world at present. Countries in the Middle East, some Communist bloc nations, and many of those in the Third World do not favor U.S. politics and attitudes, and therefore often single out traveling Americans for abuse. In case of hijackings, it is usually the U.S. passport holder who is in the most danger.

One of the reasons for preparing this book was in response to the need of many U.S. citizens who travel abroad to ensure their safety by means of obtaining a "foreign" passport.

Life After the Green Card

We shall return to the fulfillment of the American Dream shortly. We will also take a look at the means of obtaining permanent residency and citizenship.

But first, we will offer suggestions to those who just want to do business in the U.S. and need the option of staying for lengthy periods in the country which has almost impenetrable immigration barriers. There is a good reason for settling for this option. As of this writing, chances for receiving an American passport have fallen drastically. In May, 1987 a new immigration law came into effect. "The Immigration Reform and Control Act of 1986" granted a general amnesty to all persons who resided illegally in the U.S. for a long and continuous period and worked without proper authorization.

The impact of this act will be felt in the years to come in addition to the immediate relative political asylum and refugee categories. The U.S. permits certain relatives and workers in the amount of 270,000 people entry each year for the purpose of gaining permanent residency. The quota for each country is limited to 20,000 people and dependencies such as Hong Kong is limited to 600 persons a year. With permanent residency comes the famous "green card" which grants the right to seek employment in the U.S.

Under the quota system priorities are given to immigrants who have relatives already in the U.S. Eighty per cent of residencies issued have been due to family connections. The bulk of the remaining twenty per cent are comprised of those who are skilled professionals and skilled workers.

As a result of the amnesty program and after a couple of years required to obtain citizenship the new immigrants can bring their families, who are automatically entitled to "green cards." Later, they will request a broader unification of family and bring in other relatives.

Another snag is that the route to U.S. citizenship is strictly enforced and few deviations form the set course are allowed.

Any changes in procedure can cause official inquiries and investigations and can risk permanent cancellation of all applications and documents already issued.

Another result of the new immigration law is that heavy penalties can now be levied on people and firms who employ illegal workers. Those aliens caught within proper work permits will be immediately processed for deportation. There are greater chances of finding these illegal aliens because the U.S. Immigration and Naturalization Service (INS) has greatly improved its tracking capabilities.

The Other Side of the Visa

The U.S. issues 31 types of temporary visas. Some of them

are exactly suited for the business person, developer, investor, trader, etc. It doesn't matter if one is self employed, a small business owner or a top executive of a large corporation.

These visas are granted for limited periods with options to renew under certain conditions. Some visas enable the bearer to apply for permanent residency in the U.S. As we will show, a permanent residency request can make things quite complicated.

The advantages of a temporary visa are great. For those who regard the U.S. as an economic focal point and who have no wish to immigrate these visas grant easy access to America without too much red tape. They afford the opportunity to reside in the U.S. for few years, unlimited entries and exits at any time.

The B-1 Business Visa

This highly regarded visa is issued to whoever wishes to do business in the U.S. The law does not define "business." Almost everything is reasonable in making the application. This visa is given for a year, with the option of extending it for another six months. The applicant must prove that the core of his or her business is outside of the U.S. and that after completion of business, the visa holder will return to the home country. Simultaneous applications for a business visa and permanent residency can not be made. Family members can accompany the business visa holder on their own regular tourist visas.

The E-1 Treaty Trader Visa

This visa is given to those who establish trading ties between the U.S. and another country. In order to obtain this type of visa the applicant must be a citizen of a country that has an agreement with the U.S. called the "Treaty of Commerce and Navigation." A number of countries are signatories. The business in question must be regarded highly in the trade connections between the countries and the applicant must be of a senior position, and most importantly, the firm must prove that at least 51% of trade will involve the country and the U.S. The U.S. authorities will check the financial side of the proposal and verify its seriousness. Therefore, proper documentation is essential. Americans regard "trade," in a broad sense encompassing international banking, insurance, transportation, communications, travel agencies, sales and information services. Not included are advertising or general trading or consulting services.

The E-1 visa is granted for four years, with an option of extension for another year. More extensions can be made depending on the individual case. While holding this visa an application can be made for permanent residency, but this would eliminate the option to extend the visa.

The E-2 Treaty Investor Visa

This visa enables the business person entry for purposes of investing as a developer. It is limited to citizens from countries which have a mutual development agreement with the U.S.

The investor must have at least 51% ownership of the investing company. A lesser percentage could be held, but, in any case, the investor must be the primary shareholder. The field of investment must fit with American industry's needs. However, one could invest in a minor business—a restaurant, office, or service firms—as long as the company supplies jobs. The applicant must reside for the entire period in the U.S. to handle the affairs of the enterprise closely. In this case, as well, the visa is issued for four years with a one year extension option. If the circumstances warrants, the visa can be extended for an additional period. Here again, one can apply for residency, but it might harm the visa extension option.

The L-1 Intra Company Transfer Visa

This visa is issued to top executives of the international companies who have the ability of operating a branch in the U.S. or to persons with specialized knowledge need by the organization in the U.S. The L-1 visa is to help organizations, developers, and businesses set up their employees in the U.S. The American thinking is that these are key people who advance and encourage the local business.

Whoever applies for such a visa must provide proof of employment with that firm for a least one year prior to the request and has no intention of immigration. It must also be established that the U.S. business is owned (at least 51%) and controlled by the foreign business entity.

In the criteria for visa qualification there are no specific limits as to types of businesses in which one might be involved.

The firm seeking the visa must be listed as an American company, but can deal in almost anything—heavy industry, high technology, information, and even real estate. The company could be part of a conglomerate or a tiny company of only one shareholder.

The visa is issued for a specific period of one year for new U.S. organizations and up to 3 years for already existing ones. It can be extended, in special circumstances, for up to 4 years maximum.

In this period one can apply for permanent residency, but beware, you will be not be able to extend the visa once you apply for residency.

A final reminder: the validity of the visas mentioned above could stretch out for decades and the advantages speak for themselves.

The Road to an American Passport

The route to an American passport is long and arduous. Firstly, a permit or permanent residency is needed, and after five years a request for citizenship can be made. Once permanent residency status is achieved one can not leave the country for extensive periods for another five years. Temporary residency may be attained through a relative or by means of employment. As for relatives—marriage, or family unification, there is a special chapter in the guide. Obtaining work of any kind is also handled in the following chapters.

As we have noted, 270,000 people make up the quota of those eligible for permanent residency for reasons we have listed. Some countries consider the U.S. as a favored immigrating country and the lines are long for visas. Frequently, because of this, it is quite difficult to obtain a temporary visa.

There is an additional burden for those seeking residency through the work place. They make up 20% of the quota with the rest reserved for those with family ties. The family quotas act in such a way that the 80% or so will always be maintained, so, for example, if a relative has been denied a visa in one family situation, his or her place will be taken by another. With a work visa the quota is fixed and if there are any "spots" open or "leftovers" from the family-related visa they do not revert to provide more slots for the work visa quota.

After some time, a permanent resident may apply for citizenship on condition that the applicant resided at the same address at least six months prior to the request. Proof of commitment to stay in the U.S. is required, as well as passing a fundamental English exam, proof that the applicant has not been out of the country for more than months a year during permanent residence, the taking of a test on American history and the Constitution and the passing of the Pledge of Allegiance before a judge. And only after all this does the applicant finally receive the long awaited passport. The U.S. does not allows for dual citizenship.

Chapter Nineteen
Blood, Sweat, Tears, and the Passport

A person could legally work in most foreign countries in two ways: by means of a temporary work visa, or by applying for work through a permanent residency request. Workers on a temporary work visa must leave the country when the visa expires. Some countries employ workers only on temporary visas due to seasonal jobs which do not lead up to residency anyway. In Iceland, for example, work permits are issued to the fishing industry, which is seasonal. In Australia, a worker must leave the country after fulfilling his contract.

In countries where permanent residency is granted for work purposes the count down for citizenship and passport begins on the first day of employment. There are countries, the U.S. for example, where one could obtain employment under both circumstances, but it is clear that a temporary work visa will not lead to a passport.

This section of the guide is dedicated to those who don't have the means to invest in order to obtain a passport. If the possibility of an investment were possible, but the preference was to labor in a foreign country in order to achieve the passport, or if a person who has the capital, but the intended country does not issue passports to investors—like the U.S., then one must take note that hard labor will produce the goods, but the "red tape" can be very tangled and complicated.

Every country protects their own workers before outsiders. Therefore, having a foreign worker status is very difficult. It is possible when there is a shortage of workers in a particular field, and firms look abroad for trained people.

A basic problem is making contact. A majority of countries prefer the contact to occur outside of their borders. This means that the person must apply to the diplomatic embassy in his or her home country, or anywhere else with the proper papers approved by the foreign employer and the authorities. As a result, this initial stage is already quite troublesome.

Mutual relationships and close contacts between some countries have developed regional work markets. For example, the E.E.C. (the 12 member countries in Europe) provides its citizens with equal working and living opportunities on the entire continent. A worker from Italy has the same labor rights as local Belgian workers. On the other hand, a temporary worker is on a secondary level to E.E.C. citizens when competing for work spots across the continent.

In 1983 a work market was approved in Scandinavia between Iceland, Denmark, Finland, Norway, and Sweden. Citizens of these five countries have an advantage over foreigners for jobs. Sweden is open for foreigners, but the competition is fierce because of the invasion from the rest of Scandinavia. In South America there are also regional agreements which give preference to local workers over foreigners. New Zealand, a typical immigration country does not have this problem and needs new professionals in many fields, including qualified people in the areas of accountants, nurses, print workers, and welders.

People with special professions which are in demand are better off, even in countries who ordinarily are not receptive to foreigners. In Britain, for instance, opening a branch office of any kind rewards the business person a work permit. And every country has their own set of standards and priorities.

The inevitable conclusion is that obtaining a job abroad is the result of various contacts—personal, social and professional. Usually, a thorough check in foreign newspaper's classified advertisements is not sufficient.

Most people, seeking work abroad which will enable them to obtain a passport, refer to the U.S. even when there are other attractive alternatives. Generally speaking, most of the flow is initially to classic immigration countries, and then to Europe, led by Britain, and then to South America, and finally also to those specific countries which supply work for foreigners. There are well those who head for tough seasonal jobs that are well paid or to positions offered by international companies, including opportunities in Africa.

Let's take a look at ways of penetrating the U.S. for permanent residency by means of the work route. We won't get into the paperwork required because it differs between professions and states in the U.S. and different employees. We refer to the those included in the 270,000 people quota eligible for permanent residence. They reach approximately

60,000 and the American authorities consider positively only three types of request: a professional in a certain field, an outstanding individual in the sciences or arts, and thirdly, a killed or unskilled worker.

Before we explain the differences, we stress that some of the workers will be accepted in the U.S. as permanent residents regardless of local work visas and without bureaucratic hardships. These are types of work that bear no influence on the American labor market and appear on chart A: operating surgeons, nurses, outstanding individuals in the sciences and the arts, especially in stage professions, religious workers from priest to Buddhist monk, to mosque employee, and executives—board members, shareholders of international companies that must be listed in the U.S. at least one year prior to the request.

In contrast, people from some professional occupations will never be granted work visas. These are typified by low education and small salaries. Jobs which fit this category, for example, are elevator operators, gardeners, concierges, gas station attendants, guards and truck drivers.

We'll return to the three categories mentioned earlier.

Professionals include: architects, engineers, lawyers, or teachers. Some of these professions require an authorization from the local employer. An outstanding individual in the sciences or arts must show proof that a certain American employer needs his or her services. And the applicant must show evidence of the special talents of abilities. It is possible to present newspaper clippings or professional essays and there is no need for academic documents. Americans also accept musicians, writers and athletes, but they must demonstrate that their special talents will benefit the U.S. economy, society, or culture.

The American immigration authorities will approve permanent residency to a worker, skilled or unskilled, whose occupation is in need due to shortage of local labor. The worker must also show the employer's demand statement. Vocations under this category include au-pairs, housekeepers, cooks, mechanics, diamond industry workers plumbers, and painters.

Chapter Twenty
Marriage for Passport

The most efficient method of obtaining a passport is by marrying a local citizen. This usually produces immediate permanent residency and a citizenship which leads to a passport in a much shorter period then is required.

The differences between countries are in regards to the gender of the applicant, or the period between the marriage and receiving the passport. Some countries show preference for men over women and express this with different time frames required for citizenship. Some countries demand, after marriage, a certain residential period. Some are satisfied with a formal registration with the nearest diplomatic representative. Children of the foreign spouse, under 18 or 21 years of age, can be included in the application for citizenship of the parent.

Many individuals have undergone the process of marriage in order to obtain citizenship. But just after obtaining the passport two problems might occur: the first, if fraud is found and revealed, all rights and privileges are canceled and legal charges may be lodged. Secondly, the partner in the marriage might fall in love with someone else and breach the agreement (of convenience). It is therefore advisable to take a reliable partner who will not be likely to ruin the deal!

Whoever intends on getting married out of love regardless of the side benefits could skip this chapter. It is for those who intend to obtain their passports through marriage.

The marriage could take place anywhere. When two people of the same faith get married it is no problem. It is a difficulty when the two are from different religions and want to marry in a country that recognizes only religious marriages.

Marriage by Correspondence

This type of marriage is more common than is generally known. Correspondence marriages are done by sending all the required documentation, including photos and marriage licenses to a given country. Countries which allow this process are mainly in South America. Most popular is Paraguay, Panama, and El Salvador. Mexico, a past favorite, is not relevant anymore due to changes in local laws. This marriage is legal because it is signed by a judge. But this is a critical issue, because in the future the legal status of this document could change and it might not be recognized anymore.

The price of a marriage license differs from country to country. (Check with the local diplomatic representative.)

The following examples will make it clearer. They're listed alphabetically and are from the classic immigration countries. Most are of Europe and countries of the third world.

Argentina: One can obtain a passport after an undefined period. Every case is treated individually.

Australia: The one who wants to marry an Australian citizen does not have to have a permanent residency status but must submit a request which would be studied by the authorities. Only after two years can a request for citizenship be made. In the past it was mandatory to live there. Another way to become eligible for permanent resident status is to prove that you lived for at least one year in a common law relationship with a member of the opposite sex who is an Australian citizen.

Austria: Does not distinguish between male or female. What counts is that one of the two resided in Austria prior to the marriage. Marriage will lead to citizenship if the couple were married at least a year before applying and one of them had to live in Austria for four years—or having been married two years before application and one of them resided for three years. Another option is being married five years and one of the couple is an Austrian citizen for at least ten years. In any case, that is a short cut in a country which grants citizenship only after ten years.

Belgium: Marriage does not automatically result in citizenship and a passport. There is a definite time period of residency required. Check the latest information with the Belgian authorities.

Brazil: Marriage does not grant a passport, only documents of lesser importance.

Britain: Marriage enables permanent residency and citizenship in three years instead of five and a half. The law is easier towards women who are to marry British subject, even if they are only permanent residents. The requirement for foreign men is that they wed only female citizens in order to have a reduction in the number of years required for permanent residency and citizenship.

Canada: Marriage does lead to a passport, but there is an obligation to live in Canada three of out four years normally required for citizenship.

Chile: No short cuts.

Colombia: There are considerations, but one must reside in the country though less than the five years normally required.

Costa Rica: Marriage results in a passport, but it is unclear just how much the normal five year period is shortened.

Denmark: Even though immigration was halted, one could get into the country as the common law spouse of a permanent self-supported resident.

Dominican Republic: Automatic citizenship is granted upon marriage.

France: Until 1973 automatic citizenship was issued to women who married French men. Today, it is no longer the case. Men who marry French women can apply and receive citizenship in a couple of months. The application can be made through any French embassy in the world.

Germany: Each request is handled separately. Usually, the foreign spouse gets a temporary residency status which becomes permanent if the marriage is intact in three years.

Greece: Citizenship through marriage can be obtained, but just how much it shortens the three year residency period is unclear.

Guatemala: Marriage does not have a big effect on the five years needed for citizenship.

Holland: Applications for citizenship can be submitted after three years of residency.

Honduras: Instead of a three year wait for citizenship, marriage provides for a cut to one and a half years.

Ireland: A request for citizenship could be filed after three years instead of four. A request for permanent residency can be immediately submitted after marriage.

Italy: Automatic citizenship is issued upon marriage to an Italian citizen.

New Zealand: Application for citizenship after a short period of permanent resident, which is shorter than the three year minimum required.

Norway: Citizenship is granted normally after five years residency instead of seven.

Panama: Marriage shortens the period from five to three years, without the obligation of actual residence in the country.

Peru: No time saving here. Newlyweds must live at least two years like ordinary citizenship applicants.

Philippines: A woman who marries a Philippine citizen receives an immigration permit which shortens the time for citizenship. A man who marries a Philippine shortens the period from ten years to five.

South Africa: Marriage does not entitle to automatic citizenship.

Spain: Marriage entitles a newlywed foreigner to a passport. The time needed depends on the person and his or her origin. In any case it is shorter than the ten years normally required for citizenship.

Sweden: The same as in Costa Rica.

Switzerland: Application for citizenship after marriage can be made in five years instead of ten.

Turkey: Marriage helps, but not always. A woman who marries a Turk is granted citizenship with a month.

Uruguay: Marriage does not automatically result in citizenship.

USA: The foreign spouse of an American citizen married at least three years can become a citizen after completing all the requirements. Instead of residing in the U.S. for 5 years (of that 30 months of physical residence in the United States) one can reside for only three years after obtaining a permanent residency and before applying for citizenship. Actually, one who marries an American citizen could reside in America only 18 out of the 30 months. Those who marry an American citizen and reside outside of the U.S. are entitled to citizenship only if they submit a request to a legal registrar that handles immigration matters. There is another condition: They must reside in the U.S. for a certain period after requesting permanent residency. It would be hard to imagine that anyone would pass up the opportunity of becoming a U.S. citizen because of this condition.

It is not uncommon for some couples to divorce after completing the process. If the couple is divided by religion and if there was a civil ceremony the terms of divorce are written in the agreement itself. When one party changes his or her mind or makes trouble for the other a suit is filed, to which experts from the foreign country are invited to testify. In this case, the frustrated and upset partner might reveal the true intentions of the marriage. To prevent complications, one should carefully check out the marriage partner, the residency laws of the intended country, and proceed with caution.

The price of such a marriage varies from case to case. There is no minimum amount and it really depends on the specific demands of the marriage partner.

Chapter Twenty-One
Blood Relations and a Passport

A safe and successful way of obtaining a passport is through relatives who reside in a foreign country and request a family reunification. Usually, the request is granted and a permanent residency is issued after a certain period which varies from country to country.

Relatives are parents, brothers and sisters, or an adult son or daughter. Regarding relatives of "first blood," a couple and their children, consult the previous section of this guide called "Marriage for Passport."

The definition of "family reunification" is a bit confusing; the spouse and common children are of higher priority. They are "top rank" relatives and they have a common fate with the applicant. Therefore, the unification means mainly family relations of second or third blood. not taken into consideration are uncles and nephews. Adopted family members—sons, daughters, and those born outside of marriage—are considered first blood relations.

The children of an applicant receives equal rights, but they must be under 18 or 21 years of age and many countries have a policy biased in favor of female children, even if they are over 21 and single. They are often eligible to appear in their parent's application from.

It is important to stress that the request must be submitted by the family residing in the intended country where the unification will take place. Among the forms to be filed is one dealing with the financing of the stay. No country would agree to a further burden on its social services. In every country the treatment is different for working or non-working family members, and a lot depends on local regulations.

Permanent residency, granted by family unification entitles one to apply for citizenship after a certain period. By this route there are no short cuts, unlike investing for a passport. There is one option, however, which will mentioned later in this guide.

We have stated that this method is a fairly safe and reliable one for obtaining a passport, but it is not always worth the effort. In the USA it is sometimes better to obtain permanent residency by means of employment, because the unification method is under a certain quota and the waiting list is usually quite long. It is possible that a demand for employment will achieve faster results than a second or third blood relative applying under the unification method.

Spain—Back to the Roots

There are certain immigration benefits to those who have proven ties to close relatives of Spanish heritage.

This is a special and unique category. Finding relatives in a Spanish family can result in the shortening of the waiting period for citizenship from 10 years to 12 months! These are special benefits, granted by the Spanish government to those born outside of Spain to Spanish parents. in this category are included parents who lost their citizenship for various reasons. The interpretation of this law is especially important for Jews, as they were once very respectable visitors in Spain. The issue is whether they lost documents showing their role in a once mighty empire.

Anyone who can prove that their parents or descendants were born in Spain and lost their citizenship could apply after 12 months of residence in Spain.

Foreigners' Reunion

It is obvious that one would wish to be reunited with family and even refugees are entitled to bring theirs. The problem is with a person who is in a sub-citizen class. It is not foolproof, however. Usually, the basic requirements are a permanent address and a regular job. Here are some examples: permanent residents of Switzerland who are issued annual permits and who have been there for at least one year are allowed to bring their spouses and children under 21. In France, this right is reserved for those who have resided over a year. A foreigner won't be expelled if he is married to a French citizen at least six months. A foreigner who immigrated to Belgium through a family unification can't do the same thing for his family. In Germany one could bring one's spouse and children under 16 if they lived there for at least one year. In Holland, temporary residents are allowed to bring their family on condition that they worked for at least a year and have a job for another year. In Sweden, the condition of residency and support are canceled. Whoever has a residency permit and a work permit is entitled to bring spouse and children under 20.

Chapter Twenty-Two
Passport as a Retirement Reward

Many countries welcome pensioners and grant them permanent resident rights that may give them, depending on the country, full citizenship and a passport. Even when in cases where some countries don't make it easy for pensioners, they do generally receive special benefits such as local travel documents, which is a special kind of passport issued just for them.

The warm treatment received by pensioners is due to their bringing to the new country modest capital on a regular basis and do not place a burden on the labor market or social services. They do contribute to the local economy by their spending.

The pensioner must present proof of a regular monthly income or a pension.

American pensioners often go to Costa Rica in Central America. The local government has initiated a plan for absorbing retirees who bring with them between $600–1000 monthly. A spokesman for the Costa Rican government says that $1,000 a month could grant citizenship in less than five years. According to influential publications, a passport could be issued in much less than five years if the pension is directed towards investment under local auspices. There is an option of investing by mail and receiving the passport without physically being there provided the applicant is a pensioner.

In Guatemala the terms are such that any 50-year-old of any nationality can apply for permanent residency through a representative of the Guatemalan government or the consulate of embassy of that country. The program is called "Residente Rentista."

To qualify, the applicant must be self supported and have at least a minimum guaranteed income of about $350 monthly.

Apparently these countries are attractive for Americans and Australians because the cost of living is so low. The classic immigration countries do not have similar policies towards foreign pensioners. There are no special plans for them in the U.S., Britain, and New Zealand. On the other hand there are special programs for them in Australia, Canada, and some parts of Europe.

The fact that a pensioner can enter various countries which do not recognize special business person status can open the way for "back door" business. A pensioner who can show a regular monthly income can receive documents not normally available as a younger business person. In some countries a pensioner is a person who has reached the age of 55, which is a ripe age to start a new career!

Chapter Twenty-Three
Passports from Heaven

The controversy surrounding the issue of separation of state and religion plays an important role in almost every society. It is interesting to note that secular world leaders often bestow great respect on religious leaders. This fact can be taken as an advantage for obtaining a another passport.

A religious official could be Jewish, Christian, Muslim or of any other faith who is seeking another passport in order to spread his faith's gospel.

These officials are entitled in most countries to a permanent resident status in order for them to spend enough time with their local communities. The path is clear, later on, without short cuts, for a passport. It is also clear that to get a passport in this fashion one must show qualifications of a religious official (which is extremely difficult to fake). Additionally, an applicant must also find a community abroad that will provide an invitation. After this, it's up to the Superior Being to do the right thing!

Chapter Twenty-Four
Newborn's Passport

There are those who do not seek another passport for themselves because of the effort and frustration required in many cases, but would be glad to help provide their children with such a document. This effort could, one day, be rewarded and the parents would be able to reside abroad for extensive periods under their children's citizenship. This is called "support by relatives." This is the adult child's return of favor to parents for having been born with an additional passport.

The gift is the actual birth, which must take place in the desired country. Another condition is having to live in that country for at least three months prior to the birth. This is because most airlines hesitate to take on board a pregnant woman who is over six months into her pregnancy.

Regulations and laws are different around the world regarding the newborn's status. Some countries issue immediate citizenship, some insist on an application filled out by the parents, and some require the applicant to reside a short period in that country in order to obtain a passport.

A good example of how varied the countries are on this question is that within the classic immigration countries most of them regard it positively except for two countries: Britain and the U.S.

In Britain, giving birth there was very popular until Margaret Thatcher stepped in to stop the mass flow of immigrants, many of whom were black and Asians. They were felt to be a burden on the British public because they often had difficulty supporting themselves. The result was that the right for a passport to children of foreigners was canceled, even if the parents were temporary residents. This right still exists for those whose parents were born in Britain, however. In Australia, the laws were changed in August, 1988, and it is now possible to receive full citizen's rights for the newborn.

Most attention is focused on the U.S., where a child born to non-American parents does not automatically receive citizenship privileges. When the parents are foreign and do not have permanent residency status the baby isn't granted immediate citizenship. But with the proper documentation the newborn can eventually receive citizenship and a passport.

Various governments grant rights to infants born in their countries even if the parents are foreign citizens. Here is a partial list:

Whoever is born in the Irish Republic immediately receives the rights of permanent resident status.

On January 6, 1985 Belgian law was changed so that a child born to foreign parents is entitled to citizenship, but the request and reply depend on the child's age at time of request.

The following countries grant automatic citizenship: Argentina, Brazil, Jamaica, Honduras, Dominican Republic, Venezuela, and Costa Rica. In Chile a submitted request is needed and in Colombia and Guatemala no rights are granted whatsoever.

The French require a formal written request and that the child reside in France. The Swiss, who are regarded as quite strict in all immigration matters, would grant a newborn citizenship only if the parents lived in Switzerland for a certain period. The child would be able to get a passport after age 21 but does not receive any special benefits except that the resident requirement is lowered to five years from the normal ten.

Border officials around the world don't appreciate pregnant women (in a late stage of pregnancy) arriving in their countries to give birth, especially when she spells it out. It is advisable, therefore, in countries requiring visas for entry, and if you are pregnant, try to arrive before the pregnancy is apparent.

Other difficulties are finding a hospital for the birth and medical insurance for hospitalization and the delivery. Such insurance should be obtained well in advance. Some people bring with them a letter from the family doctor explaining in professional terms the circumstances of the pregnancy abroad.

Having a baby abroad requires an eight week arrival prior to the estimated birth date. Take into consideration financing the stay before and after the birth, especially if there are no friends or relatives to assist.

Before setting out for the journey, verify all the expenses your insurance covers and the additional expenses for the birth, separate room in the hospital ward, constant doctor supervision, and perhaps a midwife.

Is it worth it? That is very subjective and each family must view it strictly in personal terms. Some consider an adventure or an experience, or even a long term investment. Even if the initial thoughts are to classic immigration countries, except Britain and Australia, it is definitely possible to receive the same high quality service in third world hospitals.

The new citizen will have duties to fulfill in the long run, especially if he is a male. Military service is usually an unavoidable obligation.

This method of achieving a passport is the cheapest in terms of investment, except perhaps, marriage. And for the child, it ensures an additional passport to the one already held.

Chapter Twenty-Five
The Universal Passport—World Service Authority

Gary Davis, Citizen-of-the-World without a citizenship, is the brainchild behind WSA: World Service Authority. Davis, a former fighter pilot in the U.S. Air Force took part in bombing Dresden in World War II. In one of his bombing missions he was hit and was taken prisoner. During captivity and until his release he had time to reexamine his philosophical views about life. One of his conclusions was that national emotions are a leading reason for wars.

Davis declared himself a citizen of the world and renounced his American citizenship. He issued himself a "universal" passport. From 1942 to 1944 he collected 720,000 signatures on a petition he issued calling for the cancellation of national frameworks and the formation of a universal government. In 1954 he began issuing universal passports which number today in the hundreds of thousands. Davis' justification for his passport is derived from section 13 of the Bill of Human Rights dealing with individual freedom of movement.

The universal passport resembles other national passports and is printed in the six official languages of the United Nations: English, Russian, French, Spanish, and Chinese, Arabic, and Esperanto as well. Anyone can receive this passport by signing an application which signifies recognition for Davis' views.

An additional advantage of this passport is that the personal information written in the passport is very flexible. For example, Davis has divided the globe into sectors, without regard to existing national boundaries. Therefore, an applicant can simply put as place of birth "Sector 5" or "Sector 6." This would allow the applicant to avoid listing actual place of birth where this might ordinarily place a hardship on the applicant.

A few countries acknowledge this passport as a legal travel document: Ecuador, Togo, Zambia, Burkina Faso, Mauritania, and Yemen. We would like to emphasize that this recognition was given at different times by different governments, some of which are politically unstable. This is why there is still uncertainty about the use of this document.

In contrast, about 100 countries recognize the passport on a case to case basis without logic. This is due not only to the liberal manner in which one could fill out the personal data in the passport, but also to the multitude of languages in which it is printed. As there are over 200 official passports, a border police official could mistake it for a real document. Even in strict bureaucratic countries officials have been known to have been fooled.

Countries that have given de facto (on a case by case basis) recognition to the World Service Authority passport

Afghanistan	Dominican	Laos	Somalia
Algeria	Republic	Lebanon	South Africa
Angola	Egypt	Liberia	Spain
Argentina	Equatorial	Luxembourg	Sri Lanka
Austria	Guinea	Malawi	St. Vincent and
Bahamas	Ethiopia	Mali	the Grenadines
Barbados	France	Malta	Sudan
Belgium	Germany (East)	Mauritius	Suriname
Belize	Germany (West)	Mexico	Switzerland
Benin	Ghana	Mozambique	Syria
Bolivia	Greece	New Caledonia	Taiwan
Botswana	Grenada	Nicaragua	Tanzania
Brazil	Guatemala	Niger	Thailand
Bulgaria	Guyana	Nigeria	Tunisia
Butundi	Haiti	Norway	Turkey
Cambodia	Honduras	Pakistan	Turks and Cai-
Cameroon	Hong Kong	Panama	cos Island
Canada	Hungary	Paraguay	USA
Chad	Iceland	Peru	USSR
China (People's	India	Philippines	Vanuatu
Republic)	Iraq	Poland	Venezuela
Colombia	Italy	Portugal	Virgin Islands
Congo	Ivory Coast	Romania	(British)
Costa Rica	Jamaica	Saint Maarten	Yemen
Cuba	Jordan	San Marino	(Democratic)
Czechoslovakia	Kenya	Saudi Arabia	Zaire
Djibouti	Korea (South)	Senegal	Zimbabwe

Many countries do not recognize the universal passport or Davis himself. The U.S. has arrested, convicted, and sentenced him. His status is unique. A high Federal court declared Davis a would-be deportee, but he can not be deported due to the fact that the only passport he has is the one he issued for himself. Davis resides in Washington, D.C.

Some do believe in Davis' utopian vision. Others, mainly in black Africa need his passport because they can not receive any other. In Ghana, for example, it is difficult to receive a national passport. In Nigeria one must deposit a large sum of money before being able to leave the country on a national passport. Some people need Davis' passport because they have been stripped of their citizenship. Ethiopian refugees, without a passport, who move to Djibouti receive a paper that allows them to reach Saudi Arabia. Also, business people use this passport in parts of the world where they do not wish to present their own national passports.

In countries where a visa for entry is required the final say is always in the hands of the border officials. If a visa has been issued inside a Universal Passport it might not be recognized and entry into the country might be denied.

The WSA passport is usually issued for a 8 year validity period, the issuing fee being $60. It has provisions for a medical history, insurances, employment held, next of kin, a national passport number, and it has 29 visa pages.

However, to accommodate certain conditions, WSA issues the passport also for a 3 year validity period, the issuing fee being $35. WSA passports can be renewed only once. The fee for each 2-year renewal is $15.

WSA issues a passport only in the name of one person. Children under 16 may be inscribed on a parent's passport for a fee of $2 per child.

In case of loss, WSA will replace a passport for a fee of $20. All fees do not include postage. (See application form at the end of this guide).

WSA's 7-language (see above) World Identity Card and World Birth Certificate are issued for a fee of $12 each.

WSA also issues a 15-year validity, leather-covered, World Donor Passport for a contribution of $300 to the World Refugee Fund to aid stateless persons and refugees.

In order to receive a Universal Passport you must send four passport photos and an application form containing your personal information. You will receive the passport in the mail in a few weeks. It is rumored that Davis can issue passports immediately in cases of grave importance or distress.

Davis can be contacted at the following address:

World Service Authority Dist. III
Suite 1101—Continental Bldg.
1012 14th Street, N.W.
Washington, D.C. 20005
Tel: 202/638-2662
Telex: 262214 WGOV UR
6502804693 MCIUW

On pages 174 and 175 the reader will find a reproduction of the WSA application form.

WORLD SERVICE AUTHORITY

1012 14th STREET, N.W., WASHINGTON, D.C. 20005
Tel: (202) 638-2662   Telex: 262214 WGOV UR

APPLICATION FORM • FORMULAIRE DE DEMANDE
FORMULARIO APLICACION

INSTRUCTIONS: 1. Mark in boxes which documents and postage chosen. **2. Sign ATTESTATION OF UNDERSTANDING below.** 3. Fill out form on reverse side in block letters or by typewriter. 4. Have your signature authenticated. 5. Send with photos, bank check, international money order or IRCs to: WSA, Washington, D.C. 20005. **No WSA document will be issued without payment or proof thereof.**

INSTRUCTIONS: 1. Marquer dans les cases les documents requis et le service postal choisi. 2. Signer L'ATTESTATION DE COMPRENHESION ci-dessous. 3. Remplir la formule à l'endos en lettres majuscules ou à la machine. 4. Faire attester votre signature. 5. Retourner avec photos, cheque, mandat international ou CRI à W.S.A., Washington, D.C. 20005. **Aucun document WSA ne sera émis sans paiement.**

INSTRUCCIONES: 1. Indique los documentos y el franqueo que desea. 2. Firme el **CERTIFICADO DE ENTENDIMIENTO** al fondo. 3. Llene el Formulario al dorso. Favor de hacerlo a máquina o en letra de molde. 4. Certifique su firma y solicitud. 5. Envíe esta solicitud junto a la foto; giro bancario o postal, o Cupones Internacionales de Intercambio a: WSA, Washington, D.C. 20005. **Ningún documento de WSA será emitido sin pago o certificación del mismo.**

For WSA use only • Partie réservé au WSA • Para uso exclusivo del WSA

_____

_____

_____

_____

_____

WSA Agent's address and telephone number • Adresse et numéro de téléphone de l'Agent • Dirección y teléfono del Agente WSA.

_____

World Pp No   World I C No

World Passport	Passeport Mondial	Pasaporte Mundial	8 years 8 ans 8 años	$60 ☐	3 years 3 ans 3 años	$35 ☐
World Donor Passport	Passeport de Donateur Mondial		Pasaporte Mundial de Donante		15 years 15 ans 15 años	$300 ☐
World Identity Card	Carte d'Identité Mondiale		Tarjeta Mundial de Identidad			$12 ☐
World Birth Certificate	Certificat Mondial de naissance		Certificado Mundial de Nacimiento			$12 ☐
Certified Mail (U.S.A. only) Courrier (E.U. seulement) Correo certificado en USA		☐ US $1	Registered mail anywhere Lettre recommandée partout Correo registrado en otros paises			☐ US $7

ATTESTATION OF UNDERSTANDING

The applicant understands that the World Service Authority can accept no responsibility for the position of any government as regards the WSA passport and/or its other identification documents.

Important: Applicants under 16 years of age must have the Attestation of Understanding signed by a parent or a guardian.

ATTESTATION DE COMPREHENSION

Le demandeur comprend que le World Service Authority ne peut assumer de responsibilité quant à la position d'un gouvernement concernant le passeport du WSA ou de tout autre piece d'identité émise par le même bureau.

Important: Les demandeurs âgés de moins de 16 ans doivent faire signer L'Attestation de Compréhension par un parent ou leur tuteur légal.

CERTIFICADO DE ENTENDIMIENTO

El aplicante entiende que la WSA no puede aceptar la responsabilidad por la posición de cualquier gobierno en relación con el Pasaporte WSA o sus documentos de identidad.

Importante: Uno de los padres o el guardián de los aplicantes menores de 16 años debe firmar el siguiente Certificado de Entendimiento.

_____

Signature and Date • Signature et date • Firma y fecha

Approximate size of photo.

Dimension approximative de la photo.

Tamaño aproximado de la foto.

Submit 4 photos and sign your name on back of each one. Color accepted. Photos are for file, replacement if necessary, and ID card, in addition to passport.

Veuillez joindre 4 photos et signer votre nom au verso de chacune d'elles. Elles serviront aux archives et à la carte d'identité ou au passeport et au besoin au remplacement du document.

Envíe 4 fotografías firmadas en la parte trasera, como en el ejemplo. Se aceptan fotografías a color. Las fotografías son para nuestro archivo, para reemplazo en caso de necesidad, y para la Tarjeta de Identidad, además del Pasaporte.

Send the document(s) to this address
Envoyez le(s) document(s) à cet adresse
Envíe el(los) documento(s) a esta dirección

PLEASE PHOTOCOPY IF ADDITIONAL FORMS REQUIRED

ANSWER EACH ITEM • RÈPONDRE À TOUTES LES QUESTIONS • RELLENE ESTE CUESTIONARIO

Print or type • Tapez ou escrivez en lettres capitales • Escriba a máquina o con letra de molde

Last name • Nom de famille • Apellido	First name(s) • Prénom(s) • Nombre(s)		
Street • Rue • Calle	City & Zip Code • Ville & code postal • Ciudad		
State Province • Départment • Estado	Country • Pays • Nación		
Place of birth • Lieu de naissance • Lugar de nacimiento	Telephone		Telex

Day • Jour / Día	Month • Mois / Mes	Year • Année / Año	M F / Sex	Height • Taille / Estatura	Color eyes • Couleur yeux / Color de los ojos

Special Marks • Signes particuliers / Caracteristicas especiales	Occupation • Profession • Ocupación

INFORMATION FOR WORLD BIRTH CERTIFICATE • INFORMATIONS POUR LE CERTIFICAT MONDIAL DE NAISSANCE
INFORMACION PARA EL CERTIFICADO MUNDIAL DE NACIMIENTO

Father's name • Nom du père • Nombre del padre	Mother's name • Nom de la mère • Nombre de la madre

I swear that my information in this form is true and correct.	Je jure sur l'honneur que les informations fournies ci-haut sont exactes.	Juro que esta información es veridica.

Signature • Firma: . . . .

CERTIFICATION OF SIGNATURE, OR PHOTOCOPY OF IDENTITY PAPERS OR PRINT OF RIGHT INDEX FINGER.
Certification d'authenticité de la signature ou photocopies des papiers d'identité ou l'empreinte digitale de l'index droit.
Certificación de firma, o fotocopia de documentos de identidad o impresión digital.

On this_____ day of
_____ , 19 _____ , before me
came_____ .
known to me and known by me to be the person who executed the foregoing application, and he/she thereupon duly acknowledged to me that he/she executed the same.

En ce_____ jour de
_____ , 19 _____ , s'est
présenté(e) devant moi _____
_____ la personne
connue de moi étant l'auteur de la présente demande, en foi de quoi elle attesté en bonne et due forme d'être conformée au règlement.

En este _____ día de
_____ , de 19 _____ , se
presentó _____ ,
conocido como el cual, quien cumplimentó esta aplicación y reconoció delante de mi haberla cumplimentado.

Certifying Official • Agent Officiel • Oficial de certificaciones

Fingerprint
Empreinte Digitale
Impresión Digital

_____
Seal and signature • Sceau et signature • Sello y firma

WORLD SERVICE
AUTHORITY DIST. III
1012 14th STREET, N.W.
WASHINGTON, D.C. — U.S.A. 20005
Telephone (202) 638-2662
Telex: 262214 WGOV UR
WSA GA 21100 10-85

Send me _____ more application forms

Envoyez-moi _____ formulaires d'application supplémentaires

Envienme _____ más solicitudes

Chapter Twenty-Six
Diplomatic Passport

Without doubt the best document available is the diplomatic passport. It opens many doors, especially in borders, airports, and seaports. It elevates the bearer to an extra "territorial" level in the country being visited. Except for extreme offenses, such as murder or drug dealing, this passport safeguards the holder from prosecution. Other benefits of this passport include the ability to move in high circles of government and business, tax exemptions, and the acquisition of instant status. A diplomatic passport is immediately associated with foreign office services.

It is possible to purchase a legal and valid diplomatic passport for an initial sum of $20,000. It is a ridiculous fee considering the advantages and the fact that you don't have to reside in the country issuing the passport. And it does not involve taking on a representative, employment, or political role of any kind.

A firm, Boltran Enterprises, Ltd., based on the (British) Isle of Man in the Irish Sea advertises in International newspapers, especially the International Herald Tribune, for this document. The company hides behind a post office box number which changes frequently.

Boltran directs applicants to two brokers that issue legal diplomatic passports in the black market. A review in foreign publications will reveal more addresses of companies which give the same service.

Countries whose passport sells well are primarily from the third world, such as Bangladesh, Ghana, Togo, Niger, Sudan, Sierra Leone, Senegal, and Cameroon. You must check if your country has diplomatic ties with the country in which you intend to obtain the diplomatic passport because both countries must officially approve of the "arrangement." It is possible, however, to avoid notifying your country of birth and still be able obtain this type of passport.

The countries mentioned are typified by the fact that they are poor and so is their diplomatic staff. A report by Boltran reveals two ways of obtaining a diplomatic visa; the first is by bribing the diplomatic staff or government officials. The other is to actually purchase the document. The force behind Boltran is Georg von der Hesse, a German living in Portugal who spends his time visiting third world countries. In an interview with the London Observer during the winter of 1986 he revealed that he had ties with various countries who are willing to sell diplomatic status to foreigners. He said that the majority of his clients are people in business. In his report one broker is mentioned: Gauston Sauzu, a foreign office official from a central African country living in Europe. Another broker is Louis Bravo, a South American who specializes in selling honorary consulship (see next chapter). From his services one could obtain a valid original passport. In his advertised offering Bravo asks that no one over-publicize his methods of gaining diplomatic passports because the authorities might put an end to it all. It is clear that if the document is legal it will be signed by a top ranked official.

He continues and says that the easiest countries to obtain a diplomatic passport from are Benin, Burma, and Guinea. But these are hardly desirable places from the standpoint of respectability in the international community. Therefore, the risk involved in obtaining a diplomatic passport from these countries is questionable and not recommended.

An English weekly magazine found that Von der Hesse's company does not deal with passport transactions but just refers applicants to others. And according to Von der Hesse, his fees are less expensive than Costa Rica and Paraguay which also supply diplomatic passports for a price. The whole concept of holding a diplomatic passport sounds a bit imaginary perhaps, but for those who are skeptical there is still another type of status which is a little less glamorous, but a bit more secure; the honorary consulship passport.

Chapter Twenty-Seven
Honorary Consulship

An honorary consulship is a status recognized in diplomatic circles, although it is considered less than an official representative. The appointment of an honorary consul must be confirmed by both the home country and the intended country. Usually, an honorary consul is a citizen or resident in a country where he or she plays the role of consul of the other country.

This role is usually as a replacement for an official diplomatic representative from small countries whose budgets are also small. There are also cases in which the title and status of honorary consul is bestowed upon someone for life achievement or service and is usually given for life. Only the breaking of diplomatic ties between two countries can cancel such status.

The rights of honorary consul are few and does not grant citizenship of the country in which the consul is a representative. The consul does not receive a salary and more often than not, must meet his or her own expenses in performing any service on behalf of the home country. The honorary consul has no diplomatic immunity and is not exempt from taxes or customs duties. The honorary consul does not receive a diplomatic passport; only authorization from the foreign office.

One benefit gained, however, is a white consular license plate for an automobile. This plate, for all intents and purposes looks like a regular diplomat's plate. The honorary consul can have some fun showing off for the neighbors.

The honorary consul does not have to speak the language of the country where the residence will take place, and in fact, doers not have to even visit there at all.

So what is so positive or lucrative about being an honorary consul? By means of this status one could enhance personal economic interests. This is why honorary consulship is in high demand. The best and safest way to obtain this status is by making contacts with high officials in a foreign country. In order to obtain Honorary Consul status all that is needed is an approval of the two related countries.

An honorary consul, in most cases, is a man well established in the local community, and well above average in financial position and social status. The honorary consul traditionally is the host of high powered cocktail parties, and upon request, arrange meetings between various commercial factors.

The supply for this "job" can not meet the high demand, so an industry that sells it for money has developed. An honorary consul title costs in the neighborhood of $22,000 because of its high economic value. The previously mentioned firm, Boltran, also supplies this kind of title through a mediator from South America. There are also other companies involved in this kind of title brokerage.

Countries which sell titles of honorary consuls are Argentina, Bolivia, Mexico, and Colombia. According to the company's representative, getting this title in most South American countries is fairly easy. Therefore, for those who can't wait, you can try to find agents who sell official authorizations and then buy one and start doing business. Incidentally, one can hold the title of honorary consul to several countries at once.

We almost forgot the main issue: honorary consul status can substantially shorten the time needed to obtain a valid passport from another country.

Chapter Twenty-Eight
Dual Citizenships—Advantages and Disadvantages

Every independent country decides who is a citizen and who is not. It is possible for someone to hold two, three, or more citizenships simultaneously and has all the rights, privileges, and obligations of each country.

People often hold dual citizenship for reasons other than immigration, such as the marrying a foreign citizen. Dual citizenship is a complex issue due to the many various immigration and citizenship laws around the world. Some countries allow dual citizenship and others retrieve their citizenship once a person applies elsewhere. Some do not recognize the new citizenship and some do not grant immediate citizenship to a spouse. There is no logic involved, and it is entirely up to each country on how it handles these matters.

Dual citizenship is regarded as an asset, but it is not without snags—unexpected penalties, tax problems, financial responsibilities, or military service problems.

Every individual must consider whether it is an advantage or disadvantage to hold dual citizenship. Another consideration is whether or not to discard the first passport after receiving the second and better one.

Dual citizens have their share of problems. If one becomes involved in legal or political problems in one country in which he or she is a citizen, the other country can not act effectively without being accused in meddling in the affairs of a sovereign state. Another potential problem is an unexpected dispute between the two countries of the dual citizenship. But the most severe problem is if the "new" country does not recognize dual citizenship, requiring the relinquishment of citizenship in the first country.

Countries' attitudes to dual citizenship vary like the request for citizenship itself. Classic Western immigration countries allow most people to hold two passports. Australia might cancel a person's passport if that person were found to be actively seeking another.

Here are a few examples showing the treatment of this issue:

Europe as a whole has no clear policy. Ireland recognizes dual citizenship, but Austria does not except in rare cases. In Italy and Belgium duality is completely disregarded. In Germany special conditions are to be met. Holland does not take any note of duality and gives tacit approval. Turkey and Greece allow it. Norway, Sweden and France do not. Spain does only with certain countries. The Swiss are a bit strange in this matter. A Swiss citizen can acquire another passport but the reverse is not true. Whoever gains a Swiss passport is required by law to give up all others.

In South America there is similar variation. Bolivia and Uruguay do not recognize duality. In Argentina only Spanish and Italian passports can be held in addition to that of Argentina. In Brazil it is forbidden by law to have more than a Brazilian passport, but in practice, there is little checking. Jamaica and the Dominican Republic allow duality. Honduras, Mexico, and does not. Chile has an agreement only with Spain concerning duality. Other passports must be given up.

South Africa, Japan, and the Philippines do not allow duality.

A country which denies duality doesn't necessarily have a similar attitude towards marriage which automatically grants an alternative citizenship or to citizenship as a result of family related situations.

Even countries which have a negative policy towards dual citizenships can not really prosecute a holder of two passports until the "illegal" one is shown or used by mistake.

As far as we know there is no central data bank containing confidential information about citizens from any country.

Chapter Twenty-Nine
Police Certificate
of Good Conduct

For anyone applying for permanent residency and citizenship in almost any country a police certificate of good conduct or a form of it, is required. This document states that the applicant has no criminal record and is of good moral character. The applicant can submit the certificate to an embassy in person or authorize a diplomatic representative to contact the police directly. The certificate does not detail any offenses which can only be done with the consent of the applicant.

Normally, this certificate is issued within a few days, but can take up to a month in some countries. If there were convictions on the record there is always a double checking and confirmation to see if there was a computer error. Despite the most careful checking, people with criminal records often elude all the checks and double checks. Sometimes this is due to an ongoing court case and other times its due to having the right connections in high places. "Money talks" is still a truism. There are many famous cases of people considered criminals in their home country, only to be hailed as heroes in another.

Some countries still welcome convicted felons with the provision that the offender was not punished for two or more felonies and did not spend more than five years imprisonment, and if the crimes were not related to drug addiction.

Chapter Thirty
The Best Advice

You, dear reader are nearing the end of this guide. We hope we have enlightened you on the means of obtaining an additional passport through investment, marriage, diplomatic status, and even being a "citizen of the world." You are surely wondering what is the best offer and we can not give you a clear cut answer. What is clear is that there certainly is more than one way!

You must make a choice which is the best route for you. We hope that this guide coupled with your own attributes will enable you to achieve your goal.

We have tried to highlight some of the classic immigration countries by giving detailed accounts of the ways of emigrating to them and gaining an additional passport.

We advise you to take into consideration the basics of obtaining the additional passport. You must know exactly what your goal is; to obtain an additional passport to the one you already hold. Whatever your purpose, business, emigration, or other, the approach to each is different and each has different short and long term consequences on your life.

Another point to consider is how much money to invest and if it is worth it, as well as to judge whether the investment will provide the pay back you desire. If it doesn't is it worth it just to obtain the second passport?

When an investment requires a residency abroad will you or your family be committed to it? If you are single, consider that you could fall in love and obtain a second passport at the same time!

Additionally, you have to ask if the transition to another country is worth the price and for a temporary or permanent stay? Can you manage changing your way of life, language, daily routine, and culture shock? A new language is a big problem. Better start learning it ahead of time so you won't be at a disadvantage upon arrival.

Still there are other questions and considerations. In the process of selecting a country, one must weigh the benefits that the country offers in terms of international status. Some of the benefits have been mentioned already in this guide. Here are some highlights to remember:

- A work permit, residency, or citizenship in any of the twelve European Common Market (E.E.C.) countries is valid in any other member country
- In Scandinavia, holding a work permit, residency, or citizenship entitles the holder to a job in any of the five Scandinavian countries
- A person who receives one country's citizenship often receives residency rights or even citizenship in another country or countries. This is based on historic, national, or regional reasons and considera-

tions. Empires which have collapsed, such as the British, Dutch, Spanish, and Belgian have left local independent entities with similar rights accorded to those living in the "mother" country

When selecting a country, look into its regulations concerning military service; whether it's compulsory or requires reserve duty. Countries in which service is mandatory provide certain rights to immigrants. If trouble does occur it could be solved legally or financially.

Many people act on a whim or out of emotion. Do not do so when acting upon the information provided in this guide. It could potentially land you in trouble!

Chapter Thirty-One
More Helpful Contacts

All through this guide we gave various addresses for specific information and specific offers. Here are still more to assist you:

Addresses of diplomatic representatives in your country, even those mentioned in this guide, are listed in your telephone directories and "Yellow Pages." If this is not sufficient you could try writing directly to the intended country. The best way to obtain information and applications is through embassies and consulates in capital and major cities.

You can also check foreign newspapers for law firms or other offices which handles additional passports. Another option is addressing commercial offices or industrial unions abroad.

For those interested in third world countries, try obtaining the British monthly *South*, mentioned in Chapter Fifteen, "Finding Investments Abroad." It carries information on economic happenings, addresses opening hours of government offices and banks, and the political state of various third world countries. It costs about $5.00 per issue, including postage. For details on entry visas to different countries about which you are uncertain if they have diplomatic relations with your own country check the "T.I.M.—Travel Information Manual." It is published by the 14 members of I.A.T.A.—International Aviation Transport Authority. To purchase the manual contact:

> T.I.M.
> P.O.B. 7627
> 1117 ZJ Schipol Airport
> The Netherlands

This manual gives up to date information on entry and departure regulations in each country that has an airport or seaport. You could very simply know where you are unwanted and where you are welcome.

And finally, if you need more information on issues covered in this guide we can furnish you with this upon request. Each inquiry sent to our address costs $15.00 and is counted as one unit (similar to the one mentioned at Dun and Bradstreet.)

Our address is:

> Nesis Group, Inc.
> Survey Dept. # 281
> Cherokee Station P.O.B. 20309
> New York, New York 10028
> USA

Please send money *only* in U.S. Dollars or U.S. traveler's checques.